RAYMOND WILLIAMS

For Makiko,

"washi no sekai"

RAYMOND WILLIAMS

Tony Pinkney

Border Lines Series Editor
John Powell Ward

SEREN BOOKS

SEREN BOOKS is the imprint of
Poetry Wales Press Ltd
Andmar House, Tondu Road,
Bridgend, Mid Glamorgan

©Tony Pinkney, 1991

British Library Cataloguing in Publication Data for this title
is available from the British Library Data Office

ISBN 1–85411–047–0
ISBN 1–85411–048–9 paperback

*The publisher acknowledges the financial support of the Welsh Arts
Council*

Typeset in 10½ point Plantin by Megaron, Cardiff
Printed by Billings and Sons Ltd, Worcester.

Contents

List of Illustrations

Preface

The Border Country is that region between England and Wales which is upland and lowland, both and neither. Centuries ago kings and barons fought over these Marches without their national allegiance ever being settled. In our own time, referring to his own childhood, that eminent borderman Raymond Williams once said: "We talked of 'The English' who were not us, and 'The Welsh' who were not us." Even in our mobile and crowded age, the region retains its mystery.

In cultural terms too the region is as rich and fertile as is its agriculture and soil. The continued success of the Three Choirs Festival and the growth of the border town of Hay as a centre of the secondhand book trade, have both attracted international recognition. The present series of introductory books is offered in the light of such events. We attempt to see writers as diverse as Mary Webb, Raymond Williams and Wilfred Owen in the special light — perhaps that cloudy, golden twilight so characteristic of the region — of their origin in this area or association with it. There are titles too, though fewer, on musicians and painters. The Gloucestershire composers such as Samuel Sebastian Wesley, and painters like David Jones, bear the imprint of border woods, rivers, villages and hills.

How wide is the border? It is two, five or fifteen miles each side of the boundary; it depends on your perspective, on the placing of the nearest towns, and on the terrain itself. It also depends on history. In the time of Offa and after, Hereford itself was a frontier town, and Welsh was spoken there even in the nineteenth century. True border folk traditionally did not recognise those from even a few miles away. Today, with greater mobility, the crossing of boundaries is easier, whether for education, marriage, art, or just leisure. For myself, who spent some childhood years in Herefordshire and much of the past ten crossing between England

and Wales once a week, I can only say that as you approach the border you feel it. Suddenly you are in that finally elusive terrain, looking from a bare height down on to a plain, or from the lower land up to a gap in the hills, and you want to explore it, maybe not to return.

The elusiveness pertains to the writers and artists too. Did the urbane Elizabeth Barrett Browning, just outside Ledbury till her late twenties, have a border upbringing? Are the "English pastoral" composers, with names like Parry, Howells, and Vaughan Williams, English, or are they indeed Welsh? One wonders whether border country is now suddenly found on the English side of the Severn Bridge, and how far even John Milton's *Comus*, famous for its first production in Ludlow Castle, is in any sense such a work. Then there is the fascinating Uxbridge-born Peggy Ann Whistler, transposed in the 1930s into Margiad Evans to write her visionary novels set near her beloved Ross-on-Wye and which today still retain a magical charm. Further north: could Barbara Pym, born and raised in Oswestry, even remotely be called a border writer? Most people would say that the poet A.E. Housman was far more so, yet he virtually never visited the county after which his chief book of poems, *A Shropshire Lad*, is named. Further north still: there is the village of Chirk on the boundary itself, where R.S. Thomas had his first curacy; there is Gladstone's Hawarden library, just outside Chester and actually in Clwyd in Wales itself; there is intriguingly the Wirral town of Birkenhead, where Wilfred Owen spent his adolescence and where his fellow war poet the Welsh Eisteddfod winner Hedd Wyn was awarded his Chair – posthumously.

On the Welsh side the names are different. The mystic Ann Griffiths; the metaphysical poet Henry Vaughan; the nineteenth century novelist Arthur Machen; and the remarkable Thomas Olivers of Gregynog, author of the well-known hymn 'Lo he comes with clouds descending'. Those descending clouds . . .; in border country the scene hangs overhead, and it is easy to indulge in inaccuracies. Most significant perhaps is the difference to the two peoples on either side. From England, the border meant the enticement of emptiness, a strange unpopulated land, going up and up into the hills. From Wales, the border meant the road to London, to the university, or to employment, whether by droving sheep, or later to the industries of Birmingham and Liverpool. There were alienating elements too, since borders and boundaries are necessarily political. Much is shared, yet people on each side can speak different languages, in more than one sense.

With one or two exceptions, the books in this series are short introductory studies of a single person's work. There are no footnotes or indexes. The bibliography lists every main source referred to in the text, and sometimes others, for the use of anyone who would like to pursue the topic further. The authors reflect the diversity of their subjects. Some approach their topic as specialists or academics, some as poets or musicians themselves, some as ordinary people with however an established reputation of writing imaginatively and directly about what most moves them. They are young and old, male and female, Welsh and English, border people themselves or from further afield.

The above picture of the borders can of course be idealised. Raymond Williams, one of the leading analysts of the politics of culture this century has produced, might have said so. Yet his own love of this place where he was born, grew up, and probably never really left, appears in extraordinary detail on every page of his half-dozen novels, most notably in the so-called "border trilogy", which was thirty years in the writing. Such affection is indeed mysterious in its very precision, as his final novel *People of the Black Mountains*, makes clear. Williams's lifelong achievement was to be unflinching in his insistence on what places and people can do to each other. Pollution, mindless tourism, rootless land ownership and other insensitivities are merely the grossest of such activity. There are others less drastic, often happier; yet, in these novels, the land beneath always survives, as it always will. In doing this Williams parallels in fiction what he achieved in his more overtly intellectual work, and indeed, as Tony Pinkney makes clear at the start of his remarkable account, the novels may well have meant more to Williams than all the rest of his writing.

Tony Pinkney's book is less biographical than some others in this series, for it concentrates on Williams's novels rather than on his life itself. Yet they are novels, and of such a kind that we never forget who wrote them, or fail to sense him hovering behind them; and that is a strong thing to say of Williams, whose very self, even in life detail, was repeatedly alluded to in even his most conceptual work. Pinkney's claim is that the novels are essentially to do with the spatial and with human use and control of such space. The fertility of Pinkney's approach, its richness of analysis and width of reference, is calculated to match this spatial tenor throughout; and we are left wondering if all country is not border country; all country has both its local image and its hidden connection with, perhaps dominance by, other areas.

This is the first account of Williams devoted entirely to his fiction. It is intended for the whole range of readers, from 'ordinary' border inhabitants to students of Williams's whole *oeuvre* at all levels and in the furthest places.

John Powell Ward

1

Raymond Williams: Postmodern Novelist

Michael Ignatieff:	I'm just wondering whether it might be true to say that of all the things you've written it's in a curious sense your novels, your fiction, that you care most deeply about and would like to be remembered by. Is that just a hunch of mine? Are they your favourite children?
Raymond Williams:	I think so.

(ICA Video)

An odd paradox confronts anyone who seeks to write on the life and work of Raymond Williams. For he is both the most determinedly local and formidably international of writers; and this yoking of apparent opposites is not a matter of different phases of his career (reputation widening out from its homely beginnings) or of different areas of work within it (a local geography for his novels, a global academic audience for his cultural theory), but rather inhabits every moment and every dimension of his life's work.

Born in the Welsh border village of Pandy in 1921, Raymond Williams attended grammar school in Abergavenny and entered Cambridge University in 1939. After wartime service in a tank regiment, he completed his degree and worked as an adult education tutor from 1946 to 1961, when he returned to Cambridge as Lecturer in English. In 1974 he was appointed Professor of Drama at Cambridge, institutionally consolidating a growing national and international reputation. *Culture and Society* (1958) and *The Long Revolution* (1961) established him as one of our foremost social and cultural thinkers; and *Towards 2000* (1983) powerfully extends his analyses from a British to an international dimension. A series of studies from *Drama from Ibsen to Eliot* in 1952 to the posthumous *The Politics of Modernism* in 1989 marked him out as our major socialist literary and cultural critic; and if some of these books, such as *The English Novel from Dickens to Lawrence* (1970), confine themselves to a national cultural framework, others, such as *Marxism and Literature* (1977), take their place with full authority in an international political and theoretical argument. The boy from Pandy becomes a Cambridge Professor and globally respected intellectual, his books translated into many different languages. But this impressive trajectory — already enough, one would have thought, for any one lifetime — is only half of Raymond Williams's career.

For if one great motif of Williams's life and thought is the 'move out', from the local to the metropolitan and then global, an equally powerful counter-theme is the notion of the 'return', but a paradoxical return that temporally coincides with rather than following the move outwards and away. During the years in which he published his first five literary and cultural studies he was writing and rewriting what was to become his first novel, *Border Country* (1960), which meticulously recreates the topography and social relations of his home valley. At every moment of his intellectual career he was prepared to return general theoretical issues back to immediate lived experience, to a deeply felt personal history and geography. Perhaps the most impressive single instance of this is the opening chapter of *The Country and the City* (1973), where the historical and conceptual inquiry into these two resonant nouns is first situated in the lived substance of an individual life — Pandy, Cambridge, Saffron Walden. In later life Williams owned a cottage in the Black Mountains and spent increasing amounts of his time there, involving himself in Welsh politics, meditating in print on questions of Welsh culture and identity, and working on the most formidable of all his novels, *People of the Black Mountains*. This was planned as a trilogy and was cut short by his death in 1988, but even so still manages to encompass some thirty-seven thousand years of Welsh space and time, of the geography and history of his native region. The more international Raymond Williams gets, the more stubbornly local he becomes, or vice versa — a paradox he himself captured in his gnomic self-definition as a "Welsh European". And it is this paradox that this volume explores, a *spatial* paradox or contradiction. How can these two incompatible spaces — a few square miles of Welsh mountains and valleys, and the giant global space of contemporary multinational capitalism — mutually inhabit each other, feed fertilely into and out of each other in this remarkable life-time's work?

Raymond Williams many times insisted on the integral unity of that oeuvre, but his admirers and commentators have not always lived up to this insistence. He has a wide following of Left political activists, of many different persuasions, for whom volumes such as *Towards 2000* or the many trenchant political interventions posthumously collected in *Resources of Hope* are the essential core of his project. But he has an even wider readership among people working in the broad area of 'cultural studies', an area his own work did so much to call into being — people for whom Williams's alertness to new cultural forms and media, his powerful reinterpretations of the texts of the traditional literary canon, his extraordinary ability to read deep social relations and rhythms in the tiniest textual detail, make works such as *Modern Tragedy* (1966), *The English Novel* or *Television: Technology and Cultural Form* (1974) the very nub of what Raymond Williams was about and why he matters. In my own case, a reading of his chapter on Thomas Hardy in the second of these books was a recovery of a shared social and cultural history which altered the course of my life, and many other readers have testified to the depth of his impact on their lives. But alongside these two projects we must set a third, the novels, from *Border Country* in 1960, through *Second Generation* (1964), *The Volunteers* (1978), *The Fight for Manod* (1979) and *Loyalties* (1985), to *People of the Black Mountains* in 1989–90: a set of texts which have not yet been fully assimilated into our overall sense of Williams's achievement.

Raymond Williams, socialist; Raymond Williams, cultural critic; Raymond Williams, novelist. But our best interpreters of the first two of these figures have had rather less to say about the third, and this study sets out to remedy that neglect. Williams himself, as I have noted, always contended that these three identities were deeply integrated. In the introduction to *The Long Revolution*, he maintains that it, *Culture and Society* and *Border Country* form a single body of work, and he argued many times thereafter that what he learned, practically, about cultural forms in the actual writing of his novels was the basis of much of his later theoretical work. Yet this emphasis, in the hands of critics who were always likely to undervalue the novels in the first place, has perhaps had an unfortunate effect. It has led to them being taken (when they have been taken at all) as little more than illustrations of issues within the political or cultural writings, as being important only to the degree that a recognisable social kernel of meaning can be extracted from them. They then become, in effect, not novels but formulae, three-hundred page fictional sugar-coatings around a stark social proposition more economically formulated in a paragraph of *Modern Tragedy* or *Problems in Materialism and Culture* (1980).

My own treatment of Raymond Williams's novels will not only be more extensive than any previous one, but will also, I hope, be of a qualitatively different kind. In parts of what follows I have made a determined effort to forget that I am dealing with a set of works by a commanding social thinker and to read these six vivid texts precisely as *novels*, in the same way I would, as a professional critic, approach a batch of novels by George Eliot or Italo Calvino. Far from at once seeking to x-ray out a deep structure of rigorous social themes, I have sought often to linger on the surface of these books, to explore their textual intricacies, to follow their bypaths and indirections, to contemplate the bafflements and curiosities they so often throw up; and if this never does in the long run bring us back to a Williams 'social meaning', then so be it! I have in a sense aimed to contribute to a project sketched out by Terry Eagleton in his Foreword to a recent study of Raymond Williams, where he notes "the fascinating outline of a psychobiography of Williams, concerned less with concepts than with recurrent images, formative fantasies, intensities of feeling" (*RW:WCP*, p.viii). This volume too will have much to say about obsessive images, fantasies and odd intensities, though I regard these as alerting us to the devious life and energy of textuality, of these novels as specifically literary texts, and I offer no psychobiographical speculations at all in this book. Many, many volumes will be written on the political and cultural writings of Raymond Williams, especially as we now seek to reassess his overall achievement in the wake of his untimely death in 1988. Many fewer, one can confidently guess, will be written on his novels, and it therefore seems important that the first booklength study of them should treat them precisely *as* novels, and not as *Culture and Society* manqué. The title of this book, then, is intended to have something of the polemical force of F.R. Leavis's famous study, *D.H. Lawrence: Novelist* (1955), which similarly sought to deflect attention from an explicit social message, from Lawrence's role as prophet of sexual liberation, to the subtle craft of the novels themselves. Never trust the artist, trust the tale, Lawrence himself recommended — a dictum I'm inclined to rewrite as: never trust *Marxism and Literature*, trust *The Volunteers*.

But 'postmodern novelist' rather than just plain 'novelist', and this emphasis too needs a preliminary word. For one thing it marks a substantial shift in my own sense of the general import of Raymond Williams's work, which has until now centred on the relations between Williams and early twentieth-century modernism. In 1986 I wrote an essay on 'Raymond Williams and the "Two Faces of Modernism" ' (*RWCP*, 12–33) arguing that Williams's debt to modernism and the avant-garde had been persistently neglected by his commentators. In December 1987 I wrote to Raymond Williams, inviting him to give a plenary address at a conference on Modernism in Oxford in spring 1988. He agreed to do so and suggested 'Marxism and Modernism' as his topic on January 14th, just twelve days before his death. In the summer of 1989 I edited the book on *The Politics of Modernism* which Williams had been planning but did not complete in the last few years of his life. The introduction, on 'Modernism and Cultural Theory', extends the earlier argument on the centrality of modernism to both his theoretical and fictional writing. In a special issue of the journal *News from Nowhere* on Williams's work, this was again the burden of my contribution.

This stress on the role of modernism in Williams's thought, all the way from his undergraduate literary enthusiasms at Cambridge in the late 1930s to his final meditations on the topic in the late 1980s, still seems a necessary one, a salutary corrective to earlier critics who too swiftly labelled his novels as unadventurously 'realist' and his social writings as narrowly 'English'. For if there ever truly was an English-realist Williams, this was more of a brief hiccough in the middle of his complex career than its alpha and omega. Yet my own polemical emphasis in the end bends the stick too far back the other way, losing sight of the element of truth in the old charge of 'realism'. For if Williams is inseparably local and internationalist at once, so too — and no less paradoxically — is he simultaneously modernist and anti-modernist. But over the last two decades, in many different cultural fields, we have come to term such ambivalences '*post*modernist', and this, I believe, is the term we should now apply to the life and work of Raymond Williams and which makes him still, in these years after his death, our immediate contemporary. Postmodernism is an obscure because much contested term, as all definitions of the cultural present perhaps must be, and I have therefore aimed to define the precise significance I attach to it at each point in my argument where I invoke the term. One feature of postmodernism, at any rate, is a renewed attention to the surface intricacy and strangeness of texts as opposed to a brisk, old-style extracting of major themes, and I accordingly offer the method as well as the conclusions of this study as in a sense 'postmodern'.

Another notable achievement of postmodernist thinking has been to break down rigid barriers between the 'creative' and the 'critical', between 'fiction' and 'theory', former antagonists who can now interbreed in stimulating new ways; and this, for me, has occurred in the very process of writing this book. An initial determination to follow the dense textuality of these novels wherever it might lead, to give 'fiction' and the 'creative' their head, repeatedly kept throwing up images, fantasies, rhythms and structures of *space*, its nature, contents, metamorphoses, sexuality, utopias, horrors, its tiniest microscopic details and its most massive geographical structures. And such images turn out not to be some textual *cul-de-sac* or end in themselves but rather point towar´ ; a new definition of Williams's general social thinking. To parap˙ ase a famous remark of Roland Barthes's in *Mythologies*, we might say that if a little textuality leads one away from the social, a lot leads one back to it. I therefore offer this study as a way in, f.om a very particular and hitherto neglected angle, to a restatement of Raymond Williams's achievement, not as 'socialist intellectual' or 'cultural critic' but as 'postmodern geographer'. I define this term in Chapter Two and intend to pursue its implications for Williams's theoretical and political writings elsewhere.

If the definition of Raymond Williams as postmodernist is new, the notion of him being a formidable dismantler of barriers in his own right is of course not. Once described by Terry Eagleton as a "librarian's nightmare", Williams was celebrated for his academic slipperiness, his refusal of disciplinary pigeon-holing, that transgression of fixed academic boundaries signalled by the "and" in the titles of so many of his books: *Culture and Society, The Country and the City, Marxism and Literature, Politics and Letters*. Such texts, like the man himself, thus inhabit — to use perhaps the most resonant metaphor in all his writings — a "border country". This country begins as an actual Welsh landscape and geography, the Black Mountains and their valleys, but then expands, as I noted above, to become an entire epoch, our own phase of civilisation, the epoch of the postmodern. This paradoxical interaction of spaces, of the local and the global, of an intensely specific, loved place and the multinational world space of the late twentieth century is itself a — perhaps *the* — postmodern phenomenon, since a renewed relationship at all levels to space, place and geography is, as we shall see below, often regarded as a decisive postmodernist trait. *Raymond Williams: Novelist*, then, as a polemical battle cry against earlier reductions of his novels to general cultural or politi :al themes; but the complex textuality thereby uncovered points us beyond itself and demands the extra adjective: *Raymond Williams: Postmodern Novelist*, a concatenation of terms of whose justice I hope the reader will be persuaded by the end of this volume.

Terry Eagleton, Robin Gable, Carol Watts, Duncan Webster, Alison Easton and J. P. Ward have provided the stin lus and support without which this book would not have been written; to them, many thanks. The dedication records my deepest oligation of all.

2

Taking the Feel of the Room: *Border Country* and *Second Generation*

" A bruptly the rhythm changed, as the wheels crossed the bridge" (*BC*, 12). This is the first crossing of the border in Raymond Williams's fiction, as the university lecturer Matthew Price, the central figure of Williams's first novel *Border Country* (1960), is called urgently back from London to his native Welsh village after his father Harry Price suffers his first heart attack. Leaving his wife and two young sons in their London home, Matthew arrives by train in Gwenton (Abergavenny) on a bleak, rain-swept evening and sets out to walk the five miles north to his village Glynmawr in the Honddu valley. The "rhythm changes", then, as the border is crossed, but how, precisely?

Perhaps the first changes we note are linguistic ones, new kinds of diction, syntax, speech rhythms, new habits and occasions of conversation. What to Matthew in London is a "laburnum" is referred to in Glynmawr as a "golden chain"; his own name mutates too, from the official, registered name "Matthew" which he has used since his student days at Cambridge to "Will", the name by which from infancy he has been known in Glynmawr. Language and speech mutate also during the days he passes back in his parents' cottage. "Your voice is quite different already", his wife Susan tells him when he phones home, "Changed back . . . I prefer it" (277). The speech rhythms of the academy or the metropolis — "the language itself, consistently abstracting and generalizing" (83) — give way to that "quick Welsh accent, less sharp, less edged, than in the mining valleys which lie beyond the Black Mountains . . . a frontier crossed in a breath"(33). That linguistic frontier is crossed by Matthew Price in a key switch of registers as he chats with his father's friend Morgan Rosser, who picks him up in the car at Gwenton station. The initial curt, tense, distanced exchanges — "How are you then, Will?", "Not bad, thanks. And you?" — open out into the native rhythms of border country itself:

> "Aye, only then after all you were late, see," Matthew said, quickly. He felt the older man stiffen, and then the relief.
> "Fifteen seconds, mun. At most. And then you come out of those gates with your head down, so I nearly run you over. Even then I had to stop and ask you the way to Glynmawr".
> "Well I told you accurate."
> "Aye, near enough."
> "And the rain, see. Wouldn't you keep your head down?"
> "Aye, I suppose."
> It was easy at last, and enough had been re-established (15–16).

The very occasions of speech mutate too. "You don't speak to people in London, he remembered; in fact you don't speak to people anywhere in England" (9). In the Glynmawr valley, however, it can sometimes seem that you do little else. When the farmer Edwin Parry first meets Harry Price at the station, he follows Harry back to the railway signal box in which he works "with the local reluctance to turn away from any man just met" (62). Casual conversation here is not just time-killing gossip but a significant social institution in its own right, as Matth- recogniseson hearing the "ritual voice" his mother adopts to tell the story of his father's illness to each new well-wisher who calls (77). The novel impressively captures the way in which, in Glynmawr, linguistic casualness and linguistic formality are not stark opposites, as they are for Matthew in London, but pass easily and subtly into and out of each other. An early example is the scene in which Harry seeks to rent a larger cottage from Mrs Hybart now that his wife Ellen is pregnant with Will, a scene which passes from informality ("Sit down, boy . . . What's the old hurry?") to ceremony ("we'll have a glass of wine", 48), without one being at all able to pinpoint the exact moment of transition.

Frontiers of many kinds, then, are crossed in a breath, in language. But underpinning the discursive rhythms of Glynmawr valley are transformed senses of time and space. The train that first brings the young Harry and Ellen Price to the village in 1920 arrives late: "four twenty-three at Glynmawr would be four twenty-seven, but by country time it would still be the four" (25). And when their son returns some thirty years later, "country time" very soon reasserts itself against the brisker temporal rhythms of the metropolis. Over breakfast on his first morning in the old home, Matthew realises that "urgency, unnoticed, had been slipping away" (73), even during the relative crisis of his father's illness. There is little in Glynmawr life that can be described as an 'event' or 'act', occupying a single, isolated moment of time. Only the General Strike of 1926, which impinges from outside, can be described in these terms, and even death — first of Will's grandfather and then, many years later, of his father — is at once reabsorbed into more enduring communal rhythms. Most of the valley's activities are governed by seasonal time, in that energetic yet unhasty ploughing, planting, pruning, harvesting, picking, storing, bottling, preserving which is the enduring material undercurrent of all the personal lives narrated in this novel. Social life is not governed by linear, progressive time but rather by cyclical festivals: the poetry recital in the Baptist chapel after which Will throws his book into the river, or the Eisteddfod presided over by Illtyd Morgan Y Darren. Longer-term rhythms are established by the time of generations, by that sense of local businesses and farms passing from father to son which is so vivid both in *Border Country* and *The Fight for Manod* or, in terms of the personal lives we follow through in the former, in those fine scenes of the boy Will growing, loving, learning and at last moving beyond his parents, whose lives then belong to a settled past rather than a yet to be defined future. In these scenes of generational continuity and handing on Williams reveals most clearly his debt to that tradition of novelistic realism — George Eliot and D.H. Lawrence above all — about which he writes so well in *The English Novel*. And beyond even generational time there is the immensely unhurried time of the valley itself as a place of habitation, whose smallest measurable units seem to be half-centuries. In the 1870s Bill Hybart's father builds the group of cottages, the "patch", in which the Prices and Morgan Rosser live, and "now, half a century later, the patch was settled and pleasant" (51). Beyond all these, of course, are the vast rhythms of geological time, which Williams later explores in *People of the Black Mountains*.

With this sense of a "time of habitation", we are passing over from time to space, of which Glynmawr also has its own variety. It is a space excellently evoked by J.P. Ward in a study of 'Raymond Williams as Inhabitant'. Williams's characters move, he writes, "as though they always fully belong where the reader encounters them". We have an early instance of this in *Border Country*, after Morgan Rosser drops Matthew back at his parents' house. Matthew sits in the arm chair, away from the table, but "his mother stayed, standing in the centre of her kitchen" (18), and three pages and some time later she remains "standing very still, on the same spot" (20). The room is, clearly, a space in which she is entirely confident, to which she entirely belongs, whose every last cubic inch she and her husband have filled across the decades with the substance of their life together; where else, the novel seems to ask, should she stand? 'Centering' is a term several times applied to Glynmawr, and seems to characterise both its space and its people or, rather, the relation of its people *to* its space. Harry Price "seemed still deeply centred in himself" (37) and, a few years later in 1926, "the life of Glynmawr was so largely centred on itself that adjustment to the strike was quite quickly made" (125). 'Centred' is part of that social and spatial lexicon of border country which unobtrusively orients us towards Glynmawr life in the opening chapters of the novel. 'Easy' is another such term, from that "easiness that had almost been lost" that Matthew experiences fleetingly in London in the novel's second sentence, through that moment when unspoken tension becomes "easy at last" between Matthew and Rosser in the car between Gwenton station and Glynmawr, to many later instances, each insignificant in itself but having a considerable cumulative subliminal effect. 'Settlement' is the third of these terms, a word with a remarkable resonance in Williams's prose. Lodging in Rosser's house, Ellen and her husband discover that she's pregnant, and "from this, suddenly, the feel of the settlement was altered" (37). The word surprises us here, we'd expected something less weighty, 'arrangement' or whatever. But then 'settling' is what Harry and Glynmawr, that easy, centred space, are all about, as the novel shows in a fine page or two describing in detail how, through his work on his vegetable gardens, rented fields and bee hives, "Harry made his settlement in Glynmawr" (59).

'Detail' is, in fact, almost a word we might want to add to this lexicon, as when Matthew looks across the valley and "every detail of the land came up with its old excitement" (75). Both *Border Country* and Williams's other fiction pass severe judgement on those whose 'excitements' are *not* a matter of detail. Morgan Rosser in this novel is the prime instance, though Peter Owen in *The Fight for Manod* would run him a close second. During the early years in which Rosser and Harry Price work together in the Glynmawr railway signal box, the former's political preoccupations constantly draw him away from the 'details' that are the very stuff and texture of Glynmawr life. He is an impressive trade union organiser during the General Strike, but often fails to trim and fill the signal box lamp before coming off his shift. He has an inspiring vision of sudden general social transformation but little feel for the slow, imperceptible processes of organic growth, whether the latter takes the form of Will Addis wanting to plant his snaps in the station beds after the strike has been declared ("planting the Company's beds is work, and there's to be no work", 102) or of the growth of his daughter Eira, in whom he takes so little interest after his wife dies in child-birth. "People need an idea, mun. Something outside themselves" (88), declares Morgan, blithely sacrificing physical detail on the altar of intellectual generality. He thereby joins Peter Owen in *The Fight for Manod*, whom a much older Matthew Price sums up as follows: "one of your immaterial materialists with so much energy locked in the struggle that he's neither physically present nor physically responsive, in any way the rest of us know" (*FM*, 138).

'Physical presence', however, is precisely what Williams's fiction works for and achieves, at all levels. J.P. Ward has noted Williams's skill at depicting both "small human actions and gestures" and larger set-pieces: on the one hand Mrs Hybart spitting on her iron ("The spit sizzled and wrinkled dry", 122), on the other Harry Price catching a swarm of bees that has escaped. And he relates this to the intense sense of active work on land that runs throughout Williams's fiction: "not just Wales or England, but *land* itself, land as the actual territory where gardens are kept, railways run, roads widened for new traffic and small-holdings tilled for whatever animal and vegetable products can be worked from them" ('RWI', 23). Such activity inhabits even inanimate objects, both in our grasp of the physical processes which have produced them and in a strange sense of 'authority', of intense right, with which they occupy their place within the centred and settled spaces of Glynmawr. Take Harry's first glimpse into Edwin Parry's farm: "Sides of bacon and long strings of onions hung from the dark beams, above rows of open shelves stacked with bottled fruit and jam" (*BC*, 64). These are not just the inert, pre-packaged contents of a supermarket shelf, for we can sense just how much labour has gone into their physical preparation (Olwen Parry is actually heating the oven to bake bread as Harry arrives). These are, we feel, objects which eminently belong in this space, which have such ease and confidence of presence within it that we could imagine them nowhere else. The farm kitchen, with its contents, is packed but not crowded, just as Glynmawr valley itself is compact but not claustrophobic:

> walking the road in the October evening, they felt on their faces their own country: the huddled farmhouses, with their dirty yards; the dogs under the weed-growing walls; the cattle-marked crossing from the sloping field under the orchard; the long fields, in the line of the valley, where the cattle pastured; the turned red earth of the small, thickly-hedged ploughland; the brooks, alder-lined, curving and meeting; the bracken-heaped tussocky fields up the mountain, where the sheep were scattered under the wood-shaded barns; the occasional white wall, direct towards the sun, standing out where its windows caught the light across the valley; the high black line of the mountains, and the ring of the sheep-wall (33–34).

"Huddled", "tussocky": this is an unglamorous landscape, and its modes of human heroism will also be 'modest', everyday, easily overlooked — a dour, stubborn strength of suffering rather than the histrionics of overt pain: "Her with cancer, and picking stones in the fields. Picking stones a shilling a cartload. I still can't get past it" (190). The mute objects of the landscape also convey something of this heroism, of a grim, determined inherence in a place that is theirs by right. This quality of belonging then conveys itself to the very prose of the novels, so that the early sentences of *People of the Black Mountains*, say, become as "roughstalked" and "tangled" as the very objects they describe:

> The headlights shone on the hedges. Roughstalked bracken, on the banks, stood proud to the elbows of hazel. Tangled holly and

hawthorn, field maple and blackthorn, spread under rising rowan and ash. Trailing greenberried brambles, fruiting honeysuckle, late briars and columns of seeding foxglove, stood out from the body of the hedges. There were hartstongue ferns and the glossy leaves of ramson, under webs of fruiting vetch (*PBM*, I, 3).

"Proud" is exactly right; these are 'full' objects in a 'full' space, secure and centred. The contrast with the London Matthew Price has just left could hardly be more stark. "They had walked, endlessly, around a London still strange to them both. Their direction, always, was from a large street into a smaller, until they were virtually lost and had to ask their way back" (10).

The language, space and time of the city, the language, space and time of the country; and never the twain shall meet. Yet it was one of the key lessons of Williams's own *The Country and the City* that this dichotomy is more apparent than real. In most sixteenth and seventeenth-century literature, "the 'town and country' served", he argues, "to promote superficial comparisons and to prevent real ones" (*CC*, 71). With this caveat in mind, I propose we return to border country, to its settled physical objects and full but uncluttered topography, in a more suspicious frame of mind. We should ask, in particular, whether the hollowness and restlessness of London space do not, in fact, insidiously operate in the Welsh valley which seems so confidently their opposite.

A suggestive starting point might be the scene in which Ellen Price is 'centred' in her kitchen. Unassailable she may seem, but consider the two men sitting with her. Morgan Rosser "sat on the edge of the hard chair between the table and the sink", and seems to belong too little to this room, being as constrained in it as Ellen is confident (*BC*, 17). 'Edges' are a recurrent motif in *Border Country*, from Matthew Price's arrival at Gwenton station — noting the wooden awning and "glancing up at the fret-work pattern of its edge" (13) — onwards. Edges are precisely the point where the "fullness" or presence of an object passes over into emptiness, where it ceases to be itself; and their fascination in the novel may well imply that objects in Glynmawr valley have a less robust ontological status than a too sharp contrast between England and Wales, metropolis and valley, suggests.

If Morgan Rosser perches on the edge of a hard chair, Matthew Price slumps into a soft one, the "arm-chair, away from the table".

If Rosser belongs to the room too little, hollowing its plenitude out, Matthew belongs to it 'too much', experiencing it as a vortex or whirlpool which sucks him ever deeper in. He has already felt this kind of compression and claustrophobia in Rosser's car: "Matthew hesitated, and got into the car. Morgan leaned across him heavily, and pulled the door shut . . . It is like that, this country; it takes you over as soon as you set foot in it" (14–15). When Matthew gets out of the kitchen arm-chair, "he took his pipe from a pocket, and with his knife began poking the dead ash into his palm" (20), just as years earlier he had been absorbed by his father cleaning his acetylene lamp: "He heard the bowl of the lamp being tapped on the edge of the brick path, and looked down at the spent grey dough of the carbide". The fascination of such gestures, surely, is that of prising objects out of a space that is too powerful, that sucks and sticks and clings and will not release them; it is as if Matthew with his knife is scraping himself out of the depths of the armchair rather than just ash from a pipe. Thus even a room which affords us an impressive example of centred Glynmawr space is in fact more complex and disturbing than the London-Wales contrast allows. Settled it may be, but the Glynmawr valley is in places too 'thin', full of edges without whole objects to belong to, and elsewhere too 'thick', full of objects so magnetic that they'll never let you climb out anywhere near an edge again.

It seems to me that this account of Ellen's kitchen, which finds it a much more disturbing space than it initially appeared, can be generalised to apply to Williams's border country in its entirety. And I wish, for a few pages more, to pursue this case through particular examples, focusing on space rather than on time and language (though I suspect that a simple city/country contrast would break down there too). In this way, I hope that a concrete 'feel' for the troubled spaces of border country will emerge for the reader, before we shift dimension to ask about the theoretical and political significance of such spaces. My second example is a 'container' almost as central to Will's early life as his mother's kitchen: his father's signal box, no doubt modelled on that in which Raymond Williams's own father worked. For "it was almost a part of home, this box in which for thirty-six years Harry had spent almost a third of his life" (139). Already our everyday sense of space is vaguely troubled. The territorial demarcations by which we make sense of our lives — private versus public, home versus work — seem not to map very usefully on to Will's village, where the concept of 'home' expands to encompass whole tracts of what we can then no longer simply call 'public' space. The signal box is a key instance of this process, though there are others, as we shall see.

After his father's heart attack, Matthew goes to the box to bring home Harry's possessions. As he opens the outer door, he finds himself "in the little square between two doors, and the place came back to him" (139). This too is faintly odd. It is in a place which is not a place, which is spatially indeterminate because it is neither truly inside the signal box nor simply outside in the external world, that the actuality of place "comes back" to Matthew. Just as the edges of objects absorb *Border Country*, so too is it the margins and supplements of a space, rather than the space itself, which here and elsewhere stir Williams's imagination at every level. The geographical paradox of a "border country" — how can a country be a border? borders are what countries have, not what they are — is pursued on a descending scale into every last building, room, nook, coign or cupboard. In our conventional thinking, the room or territory seems the central, substantial reality, and its borders strike us as secondary and derivative. But a moment's further thought unsettles our complacency. For it is only by drawing a border, scratching a line in the sand or mud, that that supposedly original space comes into being in the first place. The room or country is constituted *by* its border; it turns out to be secondary to that which was supposed to be secondary to it or, we could even say, it becomes the border of its own border. Such spatial paradoxes, where we can no longer with any confidence say what is inside and what is outside, are at every textual level the very stuff of Raymond Williams's fiction.

Fringed by an indeterminate space, the signal box contains its own vivid spaces, of both desire and taboo. The latter is represented by Harry's locker:

> Matthew took Harry's keys from his pocket, and bent and opened the locker. The bottom was filled with cotton waste and a big roll of brown corrugated paper. On the shelf were the usual possessions: the stump of yellow comb, the glass jar of tea and sugar, the blue cap, the rule-book, the old bone-handled razor, the pencil and signal pad, the spare spectacle case, the heap of saved string. He stared over them, not knowing what to do (140).

In his fine study of *The Poetics of Space*, Gaston Bachelard ponders "images which may be considered to be the houses of things: drawers, chests and wardrobes. What psychology lies behind their locks and keys! They bear within themselves a kind of aesthetics of hidden things" (*PS*, xxxiii). Bachelard's sense of the power of such intimate cubby-holes is shared by Harry's workmate Jim Price, for whom "the privacy of the lockers was absolute" (140) — a taboo which only a son dare violate. Yet Jim's intensity only highlights Matthew's spatial anaesthesia. This penetration of the father's secret enclosures might be expected to arouse a whole host of psychoanalytical effects (and does when Peter Owen steals his father's car in *Second Generation*), but is here carried out mechanically, in a mode of neutral, precise, 'camera-eye' registration. In this item-by-item listing of Harry Price's possessions, the novel risks boring or alienating us by its sheer thoroughness, its drive to omit nothing from its inventory; but the alienation, clearly, is Matthew's before it is the reader's. Still essentially out of touch with his father despite the latter's physical suffering, the son can make no sense of the objects in the locker, cannot in any way see them (to borrow Williams's own definition of culture) as aspects of a "whole way of life". We as readers, however, can restore these objects to their living contexts, can make of them "details" which "come up with their old excitement" as they so clearly do not in Matthew's inert encyclopaedia. The heap of saved string testifies to the father's thrift and general handiness ("the hairy white string he always carried", 197); it is a tiny index of that massive "strength" the son grows up protected by, even if he later resents and challenges it. The bone-handle of the razor points towards a striking "poetry of handles" which I shall show at work in both *Border Country* and *Second Generation*, but which seems unable fully to emerge in these lines. The jars of tea and sugar recall that momentous last cup of tea that Harry makes for his son in the box just before Will's departure for Cambridge University. But to the grown man Matthew these potent tokens and symbols of his early life have become so much dead bric-a-brac, museum items to be patiently catalogued. The very language of the text is anaesthetised, dragged down to the level of a space which no longer resonates with mood and memory: not 'he recognised' or even 'he saw' but, passively, "on the shelf *were* the usual possessions".

However, the episode in the signal box does not end in the spiritual aboulia which afflicts Matthew here: he proceeds to 'take' the train from Pont Dulas, operating the box and once more deeply entering the physical rhythms of its work. The key transition from detached description to participation is again an experience of space:

> Matthew looked round the box. He recognized the flap-table, under the little window, where he had hidden when his father teased him, saying the Inspector was coming, or when his mother had got off the train and been told he was lost (140).

Far from collecting items from a locker, Matthew is now an object inside one. As a site of nestling concealment and childish delight, the flap-table magically transforms public working space back into an "extension of the home". We are here in the presence of what Gaston Bachelard terms an "image of felicitous space", "eulogized space", whose full-scale study would, he argues, found the science of "topophilia" (*PS*, xxxi). A related instance of felicitous space is the hide-out that Will and his friends later discover: "Elwyn helped Will out through the narrow passage from their hide under the holly bush" (108), the first of many "nests" in Raymond Williams's novels. Once Matthew rediscovers the stirring utopian space of the flap-table, the one cranny of subjectivity in the bleached, uninvolving waste that Glynmawr has become to his adult, educated self, he feels his way back bit by bit into relation with the signal box itself, and recovers a Proustian *temps perdu* or lost time when he leans out of the window in a characteristic stance of his father's. For as Bachelard cryptically puts it, "in its countless alveoli space contains compressed time. That is what space is for" (*PS*, 8).

But even the most 'positive' spaces of border country, like Ellen's kitchen, have disturbing undertones, and this is again true here. Raymond Williams's grasp of "eulogised space" is more complex than Gaston Bachelard's, and this for two reasons. The joy of invisibility, of the child's hiding, is notably double-edged in *Border Country*. Ellen Price may be told in jest that her son is "lost", but then as an adult he is so still, and now in deadly earnest. Alienated from both parents and community by his educational trajectory from Gwenton grammar school through Cambridge

28

University to academic career, his 'invisibility' is no longer a game but a jarring social affliction. This is neatly illustrated by his attempts after his return to shop in Gwenton, where he is so out of touch with local conventions as to be virtually invisible to the shopkeepers and to come home empty-handed. Thus the nooks and corners in which he used to conceal himself as a child point ominously forwards as well as felicitously back, to a 'hiddenness' which can't be overcome simply by crawling out from under a flap or holly bush. A second decisive element of Williams's vision of space is signalled by the presence of the Inspector, whether real or in jest. For space can never be separated from *power*, from the issue of who is authorised to be in it and who can give such authorisation. Spatial taboos may be benign or 'horizontal', as when you refuse to pry into a workmate's locker, but they may also be malign or 'vertical', when authoritarian social power draws a line you may not cross, sketching out a preserve you must not enter or an enclosure within which you must remain. Climbing into the box, Matthew has already ignored the "square metal notice forbidding entry to unauthorized persons" (139). But how can you *know* whether you are authorised or not to cross these entrances and frontiers, since only a moment or two later he feels that "he had no right, after all, to come playing at a man's work" (142)? And what is the relation between the spaces of power and what we might term, with Jim Price in mind, comradely space? Which is the 'real' signal box, the one whose door the Inspector slams in your face or the one where your dad plays tricks on your mum and which is almost part of your home?

This question of which is the 'real' box or room comes up very sharply in the novel's description of the cottage into which Harry and Ellen move after Ellen becomes pregnant. For the cottage contains a peculiar room, a room which is in fact not a room in any normal sense:

> The pantry was matched by another, extremely small room, which had a door to it from the living room. Nothing could be done in so small a space, though it had a door to it and was a room in everything but size. Harry, walking round one day with Mrs Hybart, before the move, argued that this space should never have been walled-off at all, but left with the living room. Mrs Hybart agreed, and added: 'I took less interest, see, then. I had the children in arms' (51).

And indeed nothing *can* be done in or with this room; it makes no further appearance in the narrative whatsoever. Why, then, should the novel spend time informing us of its existence? What does it gain by so doing?

We certainly can't interpret this strange non-room in the same way as the flap-table and the holly bush hide-out. It might seem that a peculiar nook that adults can see no earthly use for, a roomlet scaled perfectly down to his own tiny form, would have delighted the toddler or boy Will Price, becoming for him a miniature "eulogised space" which, like C.S. Lewis's wardrobe, might open straight on to the magical realm of Narnia. Yet there is a notable lack of pleasure in the lines I have cited, which do not read like a hymn of devotion to a much-loved nook. A second reason for the novel's interest in this room-which-is-not-a-room is its general desire to 'historicise' buildings, to show them to be not just inert given objects but rather an active process of making and remaking across the generations. The passage from which I've excerpted my quotation does indeed trace the history of the 'patch' across time, from the initial building by Josh Hybart in the nineteenth century to the additions and conversions carried out by his son in the twentieth; thus, as I noted above, we come to sense the rhythms of a 'time of habitation' in border country. If buildings are to be traced back to the desires, hopes and fears of their builders, then the useless non-room here testifies to the personal ineffectuality of Bill Hybart, its perpetrator; and as her closing comment suggests, his formidable wife certainly sees it in such a light. Yet we remain unsatisfied. Hybart is too minor a character, and has been too thoroughly satirised already, for us to believe this could be the novel's chief purpose at this point.

A room in which "nothing could be done" has, surely, a sinister ring to it, a sense of chill and deathliness. And since it has already eaten into the family's living space, it can seem to be an encroaching spatial paralysis which might one day gobble up the entire cottage. This weird non-space is a supplement to the main living room, as the passage between the inner and outer doors was to the signal box. But whereas the box's margins allowed place to "come back" to Matthew, this margin seems rather to take it away, to negate and refute it. How sure can you be, this unusable space seems to ask, that the spaces of border country, its centered kitchens or easy, settled living rooms, are indeed as 'full' as you think? For look at me: I haunt them and hollow them out just when you thought they were most secure; I announce a perpetual secret possibility of their sudden inversion, from plenitude to emptiness, and how can you be sure that their compact plumpness, chock-a-block with full objects, is ultimately more 'real' than my lean hollowness, which can't even muster a single edge to grace it? The novel seems, almost, to be administering to us a lesson in the 'theory of rooms', and certainly rooms in general haunt its imagination. Far from being mere backdrops to the social relations that take place within them, they are shaping agents *upon* such relations, exerting pressures and setting limits, but also opening possibilities and suggesting alternatives. If the task of modern literature, as the Russian Formalist critic Viktor Shklovsky defined it in 1917, is to "make the stone *stony*", to revitalise a sensory perception of objects which grows dim and "automatised" in the routines of everyday life, then the task of Raymond Williams's fiction, I suggest, is to "make rooms *room-y*" to reinvigorate our sense of their complexity, mystery and shaping spatial power. In my third example (after Ellen's kitchen and Harry's signal box), this fascination with the potency of rooms is signalled negatively, by the sheer extraordinariness for Williams of a 'room' in which nothing does or can happen, an 'anti-room' which denies the very nature of what it is to *be* a room in his fiction and yet, none the less, may be the secret, inner, unsettling truth of all of them.

But border country is not just a set of rooms or interiors. It involves geographical as well as domestic space, valleys, rivers, mountains and passes as well as diminutive rooms you can barely squeeze your body into. It is a space you must travel to and through: London to Gwenton, Gwenton to Glynmawr, Gwenton to the mining valleys, Glynmawr to Cambridge — a space you must traverse as well as inhabit. My fourth instance of Williams's spatial poetics, then, is the experience of speed, of space-become-active, turning into dynamic forcefield rather than simple container. The novel, after all, begins in hectic motion, with a man sprinting to catch a bus, and it knows that speed and motion are social as well as spatial — or, in a term I shall often use in this volume are 'socio-spatial' — realities. To run, in London, is almost to see your body mutate racially, as when Matthew bumps into the West Indian conductress as he leaps on to the bus and they exchange greetings "with an easiness that had almost been lost" (9). Running for a bus, like so much else in this novel, is an indeterminate kind of action, a margin or border which cannot be categorised into the settled spaces of work or home; and once you enter this liminal state or 'between' you at once meet other liminal figures — in this case a representative of the early post-war black immigrant generations in Britain. It is the black conductress, it seems, who sets Matthew's mind off on his own academic anxieties during the bus ride, on "that problem of measurement, of the means of measurement" (9) that afflicts his research into population movements into the Welsh mining valleys in the mid-nineteenth century. So that by now, on the novel's opening page, three spatial movements are vividly superimposed: Matthew's dash for the bus; nineteenth century Welsh internal immigration; twentieth-century black immigration from the Empire. The simplest everyday action — running for a bus — opens at once on to the most general issues of power and politics, on to the spaces of the globe itself, in an impressive instance of that yoked localism-and-internationalism that characterises all of Williams's work.

One of the most vivid passages in *Border Country* is that in which Harry Price's swarm of bees flies off from the drying green across the valley, when hundreds or thousands of tiny bodies move as one and "the brown cloud rose steadily higher, above the apple trees" (193). But the novel had in fact 'swarmed' from its opening page, in which hundreds of thousands of bodies had tramped from rural to industrial Wales or set sail from the colonies to the metropolis. In a novel concerned with motion on this vast scale, it is hardly surprising that transport plays such a decisive role throughout. Long before he wrote his book on television in 1974 Raymond Williams was already pondering the relations between "technology and cultural form" (to borrow its subtitle). Carts, bikes, cars, vans, lorries are almost characters in their own right in this book. They embody social relationships in the very detail of their construction (what other novel would bother to note "the high-backed seat which seemed to isolate each passenger" in a bus,? 276), mark out epochs of social history, and actively shape the social relations that are fought out within them. Later in the novel it makes a considerable difference whether the debates between Harry Price and Morgan Rosser, whose paths increasingly diverge after the latter's decision to go into "dealing" after the defeat of the General Strike, take place in Price's living room or Rosser's car; Harry seems strong and competent in argument in the former, mute and muddled in the latter.

Yet if transport systems are 'characters', the hero, obviously, is the train; and as he sits above the Kestrel just before leaving for Cambridge, Will gives us a vivid sense of its spatial forcefield:

> The trains which had sounded so near when he lay at night in his bedroom, or which had been so huge when he stood underneath the embankment watching them pass, moved now like toys through an imaginary country: like a working needle through cloth, with the thread of the trucks drawing the country behind it in folds, pointed in the direction of the engine and its trail of feathery smoke (291).

"Drawing the country behind it in folds": in the spare, precise prose of *Border Country* we rarely find two similes in an entire chapter, let alone in a single sentence as here. The initial shrinking down of the physical power of the train ("like toys") seems to be what allows Will's mapping of the spatial transformations it effects, the way it reshapes a whole landscape in its wake. But a key problem then arises for the novel. Can a map, then, never coincide with the experience of a territory as we actually live in it? Does inhabiting space (which seems, after all, the most natural thing to do with it) necessarily blind us to its inner nature and forms? Can its contours only be traced by those who are detached or even alienated from it, by climbing *out* of the valley as Will does here, so that all its details "took their place from this moulding of the valley, which could never be seen down there, from within it" (291)? Must one, paradoxically, 'betray' space before one can fully 'possess' it, abandoning its lived detail for overall intellectual grasp? Or is there some utopian kind of map which could hold together the two dimensions, our immediate spatial experience and the underlying structures which govern it? Who, in that case, could possibly be the map-maker, and how does one lay hands on this utopian cartography? These, clearly, are far-reaching questions to which we must return, both in *Border Country* and throughout Williams's work.

My fifth and final instance of space in *Border Country* concerns its use as a vehicle for more or less explicit social thinking. There are moments in the novel when the mutual interaction of space and social relationships becomes an object of attention in its own right; these tend, naturally, to cluster later in the book when the adolescent or adult Matthew can articulate theoretically what have till now been vivid intuitions. One such moment, in fact, is the turning point of the novel, where the very act of intuition-becoming-insight, of sheer bodily 'feel' becoming full social consciousness, is itself concretely enacted. On his second return to London, Matthew waits at Gwenton station:

> The long platform was crowded, and he moved into one of the few empty spaces. Then he caught what he was doing, and hesitated. It had become a habit, this moving away, a habit no less his own because it was also the habit of this crowded society. The immediate defence prepared itself, that he was countrybred, used to space and aloneness . . . He saw how over the years he had been steadily moving away, avoiding contact . . . The way of thinking which had supported him in this seemed suddenly a dead weight . . . He had to stand where he was and taste this despair (315).

In a few inches of unthinking spatial adjustment, the whole rhythm and tragedy of a class culture makes itself felt; "moving away", as a class-orientated education system separates the working-class child from its community, turns out to be indissociably a geographical *and* cultural, a 'socio-spatial' process.

England, on this showing, is a place of speed and transitory contacts, of social units 'moving away' from each other in all directions and at accelerating velocities; yet the spatial experience of English society is also, paradoxically, one of rigid enclosure (which is why the sprinting body of the novel's first sentence was such a welcome release from it). England, it appears, is simultaneously too fast and too slow. It has cut away from the leisurely, 'organic' rootedness of Welsh village life into modernist mobility but then, in a second moment, each shuttling unit turns out to be claustrophobically locked into its own private space, experiencing its closure as public class-privilege but private existential pain. English stasis can then be contrasted with "good" (because Welsh) speed: the speed of "the quick Welsh accent" (33) or of Illtyd Y Darren's "darting wrists and the quicksilver, chalk-white fingers" at the Eisteddfod (200) or of the leather mail bag that, "with a flick like a stone for ducks and drakes", the guard of the *Clytha Court* hurls at Ted Wood at Glynmawr station. And this second aspect of English space is captured in a passage where the novel's spatial poetics has passed decisively over into extended social allegory:

> England seemed a great house with every room partitioned by lath and plaster. Behind every screen, in every cupboard, sat all the great men, everybody . . . If you went out of your own cupboard, to see a man in another cupboard, still you must wait for the cupboard door to be opened, with proper ceremony, and by a proper attendant. If you didn't respect another man's cupboard, what right had you, really, to expect him to respect yours (266).

In *The Poetics of Space* Gaston Bachelard sets out, through an exploration of poetic imagery, to "take the house as a *tool of analysis* of the human soul" (xxxiii), and Williams here shows how such an analytic process might be extended to society at large. If these English cupboards still evoke a certain "aesthetics of hidden things", along with Bachelard's drawers and wardrobes, they do so only to reveal the paradox of dominative space: that it 'hides' only to display itself better, noisily drawing attention to its invisibility as a sign of its prestige and privilege. Yet even in the realm of lengthy socio-spatial allegory rather than local intuitive image, space remains ambiguous. For this impressive mansion of power (which will be literalised later in those formidable country houses that Matthew spots on his final train journey back to London) is also, evidently, a prison, a carceral space that shuts in precisely those who would shut others out. Even at its most dominative, space seems partly to master those who would master it, biting the very hand that demarcated it in the first place; and it is perhaps this deep ambivalence of domineering space that gives *Border Country* its quiet political confidence, even though the most overtly political event it narrates, the 1926 General Strike, ends in defeat. But at this point in a Bachelardian "topo-analysis" of the novel, where space in the text itself has become an overt tool for social thought, we have in effect switched over to theoretical discussion of the novel, and my chrestomathy of resonant spatial images must draw to a close.

I can imagine one substantial objection to a "topo-analysis" of *Border Country* which it would be wise to confront head on: that while the novel may indeed have many interesting things to say about space, place and geography, these are in the long run peripheral to its essential concern, which is *history*, time, the past — whether this is social history (technological and other changes across the forty-odd years of the novel's action), political history (the General Strike), or personal history, as with that "recovery of a childhood . . . a living connection between memory and substance" which for Matthew Price is the climax of the book's whole action (317). Matthew himself, the argument might continue, is an economic historian, not any sort of geographer; and the very structure of the book is historical not spatial, consisting of a series of flashbacks during the father's final illness to the years of his young manhood. And within this overall form, the novel's local method is determinedly historicist, showing both people and buildings as active processes through time, not as finished objects standing outside it. A notable local instance of this 'shock' of historicising is when we grasp that the frail, elderly woman Matthew sees Ellen talking to at the back door is the formidable Mrs Hybart of a few pages but some thirty years earlier who so dominated her husband when Harry went to rent the cottage. Moreover, history is not just form and method in this novel but, over and over, its explicit theme. *Border Country* is chock-a-block with histories, hegemonic, alternative, legendary or simply personal: the placid county history that Matthew reads in bed ("That the church at Glynmawr is distinguished by its relics", 69) or the official literary history of *English Authors*, one of the few books in Will's home ("Only here we're Welsh", Elwyn objects, 105); the Welsh history declaimed by the schoolmaster William Evans just before he beats Will and Tegwyn (" 'The Saxon hordes, what are they?' Gruffyd asked", 165); that "different history" of national politics (85) which reaches into the valley through its railway line and brings strike action, solidarity, disillusion and victimisation to it; the oral communal history or "ceremony of identification or memory" which is Illtyd Y Darren's recitation of the family genealogy of the young performers at the Eistedfodd (201); or the informal history of Lewis Price's family story-telling ("Harry and I run after him, and Dad let us go", 338). All these voices, styles, forms, all these *histories*, jostle for predominance in a novel whose own grand historical project, the recovery of a past both personal and social, will grant them each their appointed place and local validity in its own overarching temporal framework.

All of this is indeed true of *Border Country*. It is a profoundly historical novel in just these ways, and thus far the objection to a spatial analysis of the book might seem well founded. In order to deal fully with the objection, we would have to consider its presuppositions and ask just why space and time are conceived as such sharp opposites, so that if *Border Country* is indeed historical, it couldn't in any substantial way be simultaneously spatial. I will address these conceptual issues below, but for the moment want to grant the objection a certain validity; for *Border Country* does aim to identify a 'bad' space, a spatial fetishism which sets in when history is indeed repressed. The spaces with which I began this chapter were both 'good' and 'bad', ranging from the topophilia of the flap-table or holly bush hideout to the topophobia of the English social "cupboard'; but they were always, whether positively or negatively judged, *active* spaces, charged with meaning and power, both encoding and in turn formatively shaping social relations. But the 'bad space' I now want to turn to, which a historicist reading of *Border Country* correctly identifies but then wrongly assumes is the whole truth of space in this novel, is bad in a different sense, bad precisely in its passivity or one-dimensionality. Its seductive but dead surfaces neither resound with buried depths from the past nor resonate with future force; and the key word for such space — or as we might do better to call it, 'anti-space' — in the novel is *image*.

In a famous passage, Matthew reflects on the valley after returning exhausted from Gwenton:

> The familiar shape of the valley and the mountains held and replaced him. It was one thing to carry its image in his mind, as he did, everywhere, never a day passing but he closed his eyes and saw it again, his only landscape. But it was different to stand and look at the reality. It was not less beautiful, every detail of the land came up with its old excitement. But it was not still, as the image had been. It was no longer a landscape or a view, but a valley that people were using. He realized, as he watched, what had happened in going away. The valley as landscape had been taken, but its work forgotten (75).

It is worth noting just how much concrete force Williams imparts to the verb "replaced" here — not just one thing taking the place of another, but place itself becoming active and energising, re-placed rather than merely replaced; and since we have just learned that Matthew is "empty and tired", "replenished" hovers semantically in the background here too. The valley-as-image is governed by the eye not the hand, by vision not labour; and as its labour is effaced it is hoisted out of history, out of the realm of human will and activity, into sheer contemplation. The valley as landscape, clearly, is 'bad' space, space which obscures rather than both reflecting and shaping social relations, space as ideology. Such spatial fetishism is not, however, a quality of actual space, since the valley goes on being worked regardless. Rather, it is a social way of seeing, an alienated consciousness which may be painful to Matthew but can also be the marker of class power and privilege, the valley as the frozen space of tourism and pastoral. As Matthew realises, "far away, closing his eyes, he had been seeing this valley, but as a visitor sees it, as the guide-book sees it" (75). And in the powerful page that follows, history reaffirms itself against pastoral, and the static image is dissolved into its activity of production; for "this was not anybody's valley to make into a landscape. Work had changed and was still changing it" (76).

Even social ways of seeing, however, have their material technologies, and that of the image both fascinates and repels *Border Country*. Whereas most of the other technologies which so absorb the novel (and which culminate in the startling arrival of a telephone kiosk at the end of the Prices' lane) serve to accelerate social relations, hurtling goods, people and messages to and fro across the valley, there is one technology which serves to decelerate and indeed permanently fix them: photography, the technology of the image. Matthew, in fact, is assailed by photographs throughout the novel. Travelling back to his father's sickbed, he encounters the "usual photographs" in the train: the ruined abbey at Trawsfynydd, the sea-front at Tenby. History may mark and scar these images (damp has got in at the corners), but it cannot now transmute them back into living substance, as the landscape could be into a working valley. Indeed, these photos seem to implicate Matthew himself in their own deathly, insubstantial space; they "were more than thirty years old: nearly his own age" (13). When he arrives back in his parents' home this congealed space seems to be defeated ("the face no longer an image but there", 22), but it at once reasserts itself in that sombre array of family photographs in his father's bedroom. The images of Matthew's grandparents stare intimidatingly down on the dying Harry Price, and whatever vitality they once had as living men and women cannot now be liberated from this deathly technological space (for Matthew's "eyes watered with the strain and had to be closed", 23). Photography and death then begin to merge into each other — not just in the obvious sense that many of our photos are of loved relatives who have since died, but in a more uncanny way whereby the taking of a photograph inflicts a kind of death on a subject who may well still be living. Ellen Price glances sadly at the wedding photo of Mary Rosser, who died in giving birth to Eira, and yet we realise at once, from Mrs Lucas's dark hints, that Mary had never been much more than an image to Morgan Rosser in the first place. Photography kills Matthew Price, too, as he examines the wedding portrait of himself and Susan in his parents' living room: "the studio photograph was dead . . . this was the last of the rituals, this arrangement to the camera: confirm me, frame me, receive my image" (144). He later reacts with great violence to the discovery that his mother and Eira are still "meeting and talking about me, exchanging your photographs" (272); this harmless practice he finds, remarkably, "disgusting", as if there were some ghoulish element of swapping morsels of dead flesh about it. In later years Williams's response to photography mellows; he writes movingly of it in *Television: Technology and Cultural Form* as a human response to "a period of great mobility with new separations of families and with internal and external migrations" (*TTCF*, 22). But in *Border Country* photos, as the technology of bad space, are sinister and unsettling things.

The image is a dead space, then, but has an impressive power of contagion. It can turn the very genre of historiography, which might seem its precise opposite, into an aspect of itself. Leafing through the county history, Matthew recognises: "yesterday the pictures in the train, and now this: the pieces of past and present that are safe to handle" (69). Welsh history, too, is mere image for the schoolmaster William Evans, its rhetorical flourishes having no connection with the substance of his life. The valley is being transformed into images both from within and without. Morgan Rosser transmogrifies the Holy Mountain into an advertising logo, having a line-drawing of it printed on the labels of his jam jars, and during Matthew's final rail journey back to London after his father's death, a consumer society wholly devoted to the image once again dehistoricises the Welsh valley into ideological space:

> Beyond Oxford the new emphasis was evident . . . from the window the by-pass roads, the housing estates, the factories; the sharp primary colours of advertisement hoardings and petrol stations. Glynmawr, now, had gone back to a memory and an image (347).

I shall discuss this new, image-saturated culture, this "society of the spectacle", at length in the next chapter. At present we need only note that not just Glynmawr but Matthew Price too has "gone back to an image". Though he had defeated his own landscaping habits, the image seems later to reclaim him, as when he meditates over his reflection just before heading to Cambridge or, as an adult, turns into a replica of his father when he dons the latter's hat and coat to feed the cockerels.

Other technologies of the eye are less malign, producing not frozen spatial images but — in another of the novel's keywords — active *patterns*, an active construction of relationships. The central episodes are Will's dealings with the vicar, Arthur Pugh, where for the first time the boy uses telescopes and microscopes: "Pattern was the word that Will grasped at, through the crowded impressions of these first weeks" (221). Reifying at the human level, the eye, we might say, comes properly into its own at the sub- or extra-human levels, in the fields of biology or astronomy. Patterns continue to preoccupy Will as a grown man, especially in his anxieties over his research. As he contemplates the gap between the anonymous statistics of population movements and the actual experience of such movements (of which his own move from Glynmawr to Cambridge and then London is of course an instance), he is inclined bitterly to contrast pattern and history: "it wasn't a piece of research, but an emotional pattern. Emotional patterns are all very well, but they're our own business. History is public or nothing" (284). But such stark binary contrasts are an index of his continuing alienation; patterns, as the novel well knows, are also 'public', and history also 'personal'. 'Historical patterns', then, indissolubly personal and social, would be what this novel is centrally about. Its project could be summed up as an effort to dissolve images into patterns, space into history, self-contained objects into active processes of development across time — a wholesale 'despatialising' that might seem hard to reconcile with the kind of topo-analysis I undertook at the start of this chapter.

Now such arguments are not so much wrong as drastically partial, inflating a necessary part-truth about this novel into its be-all and end-all. Moreover, this radical historicist reading of *Border Country* is consonant with a major trend in Western social thinking of the last hundred years — a trend which is now, however, increasingly being subjected to scrutiny. I have already referred to Edward Soja's notion of a "socio-spatial dialectic", and wish now to invoke his *Postmodern Geographies: The Reassertion of Space in Critical Social Theory* (1989) as a way of locating the historicist reading of *Border Country* in intellectual history and of challenging the assumption that underpins it: that history is necessarily alive, active, transformative and revolutionary, while space, always and everywhere, is inert, dead, ideological and derivative. In *Postmodern Geographies*, Soja traces through a "theoretical peripheralization of space", a "despatialization of critical theory", which sets in from about 1880 and has by no means wholly come to an end yet (*PG*, 15, 38). In the early nineteenth century, he argues, "historicity and spatiality were in approximate balance as sources of emancipatory consciousness . . . Challenging the specific geography of industrial capitalism, its spatial and territorial structures, was a vital part of the radical critiques and regional social movements arising during this period" (4). The Paris Commune of 1871 is perhaps the last gasp of this early thrust towards "an emancipatory spatial praxis". For during the Commune, as Kristin Ross has shown in *The Emergence of Social Space: Rimbaud and the Paris Commune* (1988), the revolutionary workers tried to reshape the very fabric of the city, democratising its hierarchial structures and constructing new, provisional, mobile spaces in contrast to its former sullen monumentality. Thereafter spatial awareness drains out of both radical and reformist social thought. Marxism, in particular, defines the proletariat as a universal because placeless class, and sees spatial identities (local, regional or national) as either ideological veils or antiquarian survivals which revolutionary internationalism must struggle to overcome. It announces itself to be merely a 'historical materialism', and not the 'historico-geographical' materialism that Soja and others are now calling for. In the early decades of our own century, the time-orientated philosophy of Henri Bergson completes the rout of space, and we arrive at the theoretical situation succinctly phrased by Michel Foucault: "Did it start with Bergson or before? Space was treated as the dead, the fixed, the undialectical, the immobile. Time, on the contrary, was richness, fecundity, life, dialectic" (cited in *PG*, 10). And it seems to me that a reading of *Border Country* which solely emphasises history as activity and space as the lethal, frozen surfaces of the image, though certainly capturing an important aspect of the novel, is ultimately trapped in exactly the one-sided "historicism of theoretical consciousness" that Edward Soja analyses (31).

Soja's purpose in *Postmodern Geographies* is an "incipient spatialization of critical theory" (12); his book is a stirring, immensely readable manifesto which is sure to do much to advance a new, spatialised cultural studies. In it, he traces through "three different paths of spatialisation": posthistoricism, post-fordism, and postmodernism. I shall have more to say about the two latter terms, which represent the economic and cultural pathways to the spatialisation of contemporary thought, in my next chapter, since in *The Fight for Manod* and *The Volunteers* Raymond Williams is addressing these very issues. Here it is the first of these routes, a 'posthistoricist' pathway through the domain of theory rather than economics and culture, which concerns me. Posthistoricism, in Soja's view, is a determined effort to redress a theoretical imbalance, to resist the time-bound ontologies of the twentieth century and to bend the stick the other way, giving due weight to space in the fundamental experience of what it means to be human. As he phrases it:

> The first of these spatializations is rooted in a fundamental reformulation of the nature and conceptualization of social being, an essentially ontological struggle to rebalance the interpretable interplay between history, geography and society. Here the reassertion of space arises against the grain of an ontological historicism that has privileged the separate constitution of being in time for at least the past century (61).

In his effort to leave a lop-sided historicism behind and construct a genuinely 'socio-spatial' dialectic, Soja goes in search of precursors of the 'spatial turn' of postmodern geography. He turns to the work of Michel Foucault, who in 1967 delivered a lecture entitled 'Of Other Spaces'; to the writings of John Berger, our "most spatially visionary of art historians — dare we call him an art geographer?" — who in 1974 proposed that "prophecy now involves a geographical rather than historical projection; it is space not time that hides consequences from us" (*PG*, 22); and above all to the French Marxist philosopher Henri Lefebvre, author of a long series of studies on the role of space in social life, including his masterwork *The Production of Space* in 1974.

I wish (as the reader has no doubt guessed) to add one more name to this role call of great 'historico-geographical' precursors, that of Raymond Williams, and to elaborate a Soja-inspired, *post*historicist reading of *Border Country*. The point of such an interpretation is not to repeat the one-sidedness of historicism in reverse form, toppling over into what Soja calls the "unproductive aura of an anti-history"; for this would indeed allow the 'image', the ideological dead space of landscape and photography, its final triumph. The aim, rather, is to demonstrate the profound interaction in the novel of space and time, place and politics, to show space not just as the mere stage-setting or eventual outcome of social relations but as a formative presence within them all along.

A historicist reading of *Border Country*, insists, rightly, that the novel is full of false or partial histories, but then what offers to supersede all these is not, in the long run, a mega-history but rather a map. Maps, indeed, powerfully haunt this text's imagination, first through the "rail map, with its familiar network of arteries, held in the shape of Wales" (12) which absorbs Matthew on his journey back to Glynmawr, a map he'd studied with equal passion a dozen years earlier on his first trip to Cambridge, when "the lines on the map ran out east into England, and he followed them" (300). There are maps of hostility as well as disorientation, as with the map read by the officer in the armoured car as the military convoy drives through the village during the 1926 Strike. Maps, like so much else in this novel, are not just objects but active processes, and may be metaphorically as well as literally cartographic. In rebellious mood, the adolescent Will snaps at his father, "You'd got this course mapped out for me, and that was that" (239); and a great deal of such 'mapping out', of varying degrees of literalness, takes place in the book. If history is frozen into a spatial image in the county history, perhaps you can defrost it by turning the history book into a map; and Will and Eira draw up a list of places to visit from the volume and dutifully trek round a different one each weekend. Matthew and Susan, a few years later, are busily mapping out urban space: "their direction, always, was from a large street into a smaller, until they were virtually lost" (10), and that "collecting of the names of houses" which is one of their earliest pastimes seems to be a way of establishing a few landmarks and contour lines on the cartographic chaos of the metropolis. Much of Matthew's memory of his home valley is "a memory of walking", and he's irked when Morgan Rosser collects him by car from Gwenton station because the five-mile walk north to Glynmawr would have been a welcome mapping of his inner ambivalences towards this terrain.

It may be useful at this point to borrow a distinction between 'tour' and 'map' from Michel de Certeau's *The Practice of Everyday Life*. In his chapter on 'Spatial Stories', de Certeau describes the 'tour' as a set of directions or a practical itinerary: you go down the steps, you turn right, you walk straight ahead until you reach the pub. The 'map', on the other hand, is a static grid of spatial relations, a two-dimensional chart which announces the results of the tour's active operations: the pub is next to the church and opposite the post office. If we chart the early history of cartography, we see a gradual but momentous shift of balance between 'tour' and 'map'.

> The first medieval maps included only the rectilinear marking out of itineraries (performative indications chiefly concerning pilgrimages), along with the stops one was to make (cities which one was to pass through, spend the night in, pray at, etc) and distances calculated in terms of hours or in days, that is, in terms of the time it would take to cover them on foot. Each of these maps is a memorandum of actions. The tour to be made is predominant in them . . . But the map gradually wins out over these figures; it colonizes space; it eliminates little by little the pictural figurations of the practices that produce it (*PEL*, 120–21).

In the spaces of Glynmawr valley, it is the 'tour' or itinerary that predominates — with such confidence, indeed, that Welsh oral map-making is buttressed rather than damaged by Ted Wood's fine parody of it: "Wherever you go down this place, it's the same. Cross the grass, past the muckheap, over two mountains, and it's the sixth chapel on the left" (*BC*, 31). Welsh space, then, is the terrain of known practices and operations, of leisurely itineraries which contrast both with English speed and English immobility (cupboards); while the map or grid testifies to a deep-seated not-at-homeness, whether that of the still alienated Matthew or of a hostile military force. In the novel's concern with both maps and mapping out, achieved systems and actual spatialising practices, we can see a quest for utopian synthesis, the kind of brief, precarious poise that de Certeau sees in sixteenth-century cartography when "far from being 'illustrations', iconic glosses on the text, these figurations [ships, animals, and characters of all kinds], like fragments of stories, mark on the map the historical operations from which it resulted" (*PEL*, 121). I shall argue below that Raymond Williams's closest approach to such poise is his final novel, *People of the Black Mountains*, which in its narrative form very precisely turns a 'map' back into a 'tour'. But the spatial poetics of the earlier novels revolve, more typically, around rooms that are not rooms, disturbing spaces within spaces, and they discover within the very mapping of space a troubling gap or border between tour and map, the lived and the systematic or, as it were, between "Will" and "Matthew".

It is, then I suggest, a map rather than a history that *Border Country* aims to produce, though this would not be a map that just cancelled out history; to assume that would be to fall back into the rigid, oppositional mode of thinking characteristic of historicism. Nor, by now, should it be surprising that space and its forms, modes, pressures, disjunctions and possibilities structures *Border Country* fundamentally, and does not just crop up in those odd moments and details with which I opened this chapter. To close my account of Williams's first novel, I want to sketch some of its major spatial structures and rhythms, to demonstrate the deep interactions between space and social relations, especially space and power; for *Border Country* seems to me to be a first draft of a novelistic, 'historico-geographical materialism' which, almost thirty years later, will be fully worked through in *People of the Black Mountains*.

One of Williams's early short stories is entitled 'A Fine Room to Be Ill In' (1948), and an intense physical feel for rooms and buildings was equally characteristic of his work as a critic. In *Drama from Ibsen to Eliot* he located the weakness of Ibsen's *The Masterbuilder* in "the dramatic vagueness of the whole formula of the 'building' " (*DIE*, 88), a vagueness he does not allow to afflict his own fictional edifices. *The English Novel* celebrates Dickens's investigations of "the analogy of houses and people . . . where the house and the life being lived in it are indistinguishable" (*EN*, 35), and *The Country and the City* focuses crucially on the representation of the country house and its estate in English literature. And in a key lecture on 'Drama in a Dramatized Society' in 1984, Williams offers a rousing account of the spatial poetics that had always secretly underpinned his fascination with naturalist and modernist drama:

> This room on the stage, this enclosed living room, where important things happen and where quite another order of importance arrives as news from a shut-off outside world; this room is a convention, now a habit, of theatre; but it is also, subtly and persistently, a personage, an actor; a set that defines and can trap us: the alienated object that now represents us in the world. I have watched, fascinated, as that room has broken up; the furniture got rid of, a space cleared; people facing each other across an emptiness, with only the body, the body as object or the body as rhythm, to discover, to play with, to exhaust itself . . . a dynamic process when the room is dissolved, for scene is no longer external and yet is still active, and what we see is a projection of observed, remembered and desired images . . . a wall papered with faces; aspects of character and appearance dissolving, fragmenting, fusing, haunting; objects changing literally as you look at them (*WS*, 20).

With that "fascinated", we pass from measured academic analysis to Bachelardian spatial obsession and oneirism; and we shall see later how important the Gothic resonances of the closing phrases here — "a wall papered with faces . . . dissolving, fragmenting, fusing, haunting" — are for Williams's own fiction, which is far less dourly 'realist' than it has often been made out to be.

Late on in *Border Country*, when the convalescent Harry comes downstairs, he and his son sit together: "the sharp pink of the flowers, and the strange heavy scent, seemed to dominate the room.

Matthew sat taking the feel of the room" (*BC*, 310). In this last phrase, space has become an object of aesthetic appreciation in its own right; its subtle formative power for the relationships that take place within it can be obliquely sensed in itself, a shaping spatial field that will, a second or two later, fully enter the socio-spatial dialectic. But the room of rooms in this novel, that whose 'feel' one must above all take and cope with, is not the living room but the sickroom itself, that "fine room to be ill in" which dominates the opening pages. Like Harry's locker, it too is a space of taboo, the space of a psychoanalytic 'primal scene', of the child's terrified fantasy of the parents' lovemaking; Matthew "had rarely been in this room where his parents slept" (22), and his later uneasy jealousy of Dr Evans is surely not just a sexual one because the latter has married Eira, but a spatial one, because the doctor's profession gives him privileged access to secret rooms which are barred to others. Harry's sickroom is yet another ambivalent space, another 'border' capable at any moment of metamorphosing into its opposite. "Small and crowded", with its "drug-heavy air", old fashioned heavy mahogany wardrobe and louring photos of Matthew's grandparents (a wall papered with faces?), it is a space of enclosure and immobility, a room closing remorselessly in on the waning vitality that inhabits it, threatening to turn Harry into just another mute object in it rather than its commanding human centre. So rapidly is this enclosure shrinking, in fact, as if it were dwindling down to the proportions of the dead non-room off the living room, that Matthew "seemed to feel the pressure on his own face, as if a cast were being taken" (21). Yet this is also, paradoxically, a room of new growth: it is, as a matter of historical record, the room in which Eira was born thirty years earlier, and it is in the present a room in which a new, more articulate Harry Price is coming into being, a father actually moving closer to his son's habitual mode of consciousness: "Just lying here and thinking. It's more like in your job" (151). In the essay on 'Of Other Spaces' to which I referred above, Michel Foucault outlines a kind of space that he terms a 'crisis heterotopia': "privileged or sacred or forbidden places, reserved for individuals who are, in relation to society and to the human environment in which they live, in a state of crisis: adolescents, menstruating women, pregnant women, the elderly" ('OOS', 24). He claims that "in our society, these crisis heterotopias are persistently disappearing"; maybe they are, but they are certainly holding their own in the fiction of Raymond Williams, where the sickroom of a dying father — Harry Price in *Border Country*, Matthew himself in *The Fight for Manod*, Bert Lewis in *Loyalties* — is one of his most enduring images.

Yet in the end, of course, it is immobility rather than new growth that characterises the room-to-be-ill-in, an immobility that gathers force until it carries Harry Price into the bleakest of all the secret spaces this novel maps out: the "third cubicle on the left" in the hospital mortuary, a final 'hiding place' which forms a sad counterpart to the flap-table under which he used to hide his son. But if we extend our spatial vision, we see that the initial ambivalence — stillness/growth — in a sense is sustained. For the overall spatial rhythm of the novel's opening section is of spurts, sprints, accelerations, dashes around a body receding into passivity and death, a still point of an ever more frantically turning world. Matthew's initial run for the bus, Mrs Hybart's urgent phone call, Matthew's hurried train journey to Gwenton, Rosser's swift drive to the village, the dialogue 'racing' in the son's mind as he sits at his father's bedside, all circulate busily around the dying body, their external speed paralleled only by the inner and unobservable haste of its own decay. But then this contrast of speed and space, motion and mass, is throughout a structuring principle of the novel; it is both a way of marking out and, in turn, a shaping force inside all the social relations *Border Country* records.

The central contrast between Harry Price and Morgan Rosser works through substantially as a spatial one. Initially inhabiting the shared space of the signal box, their trajectories increasingly diverge. The most fraught encounters in which Harry is involved seem increasingly to occur in the rooms of his home; while Rosser, who becomes a dealer in country produce after the unsettling of his political activism by the defeat of the General Strike, more and more conducts his relationships from his car. One notable episode begins with a debate in Rosser's car, proceeds to a tour of his new factory, and ends in Harry's living room — a spatial trajectory (speed to stasis) which effectively defeats Rosser's offer of a job to Will before he has even made it. Space thus shapes relationships, not just echoes or reflects them. But we should not just equate Harry Price with domestic privacy or enclosed, inward space. For

Border Country is also fascinated by the networks men and women set up, the trails and territorial structures they make as they move across a region, and the ways these interact or interfere with each other; "the house grows and spreads", as Bachelard memorably puts this, until it becomes "an immense dwelling the walls of which are on vacation" (*PS*, 52). 'Home' for Harry, as I've noted, is an expanded concept which incorporates the cottage garden, a vegetable garden at the side of the drying green, two rented strips of garden behind the timber yard at the station, three rows of potatoes on Edwin Parry's farm and even the signal box itself — an impressive unravelling of the divisions between 'private' and 'public' space. Rosser's business network is topographically more extensive but humanly less fertile than Harry's. It begins as a relief network for the miners during the strike, but acquires an autonomous life of its own after the immediate political emergency has ended. What begins as a practical transport and communications system thereby proves to have more staying power than the human needs it was invented to serve. The 'reflection' or 'image' of those needs, that is, proves to be more real than that which it reflected, a paradox of communications which will trouble Williams still more in *The Volunteers*. But while Rosser's geographical network spreads formidably long tentacles from its base in the Gwenton factory, it is less spatially fructifying than Harry's work. Whereas Harry deconstructs the private/public divide, Rosser's Country Foods operation first reduces private into commercial space, when he contracts with the local women to buy up their home-made produce, and later subjects human labour to instrumental, rationalised space — whose vivid image in the novel is that series of ever-diminishing enclosures which is his factory 'assembly line'. "Will went out into the packing room, and looked down the length of the building. It seemed unimaginably bare and desolate" (247).

The territories of both Price and Rosser are dwarfed by that 'other history' — which is also, however, another space — that reaches into the valley in 1926. Years later, Eira shows a shrewd grasp of the kind of spatial disjunction which had also operated during the strike: "He's studying Wales", she says of Will, "and he goes to London to do it" (271). We have learnt to speak readily of time warps but there are 'space warps' too, strange distortions of a geographical field which show up on no Ordnance Survey or other map. Though the space of Glynmawr valley seems so impressively self-present, so palpably *there*, throughout the novel, it is in a sense hollowed out from the start, shot through with gaps and holes bigger and more dangerous than that room-which-was-not-a-room in the Price's cottage. Memorable though Welsh space is, its 'truth' ultimately lies elsewhere, in that "world of telegrams and anger" (E.M. Forster's phrase from *Howard's End* seems apt) which is centred in London; and this counter-space of political and economic domination surrounds and infiltrates the valley at every point, though it lies dormant enough except at certain flashpoints of social crisis and class struggle.

Hence it is that the most effective image of the 1926 Strike in *Border Country* turns out to be a matter of spatial rather than social relations or, more accurately, of spatial relations vividly embodying and shaping their social counterparts. I think not so much of the political disputes between Rosser, Price and Jack Meredith in the signal box, though these are tense enough; nor of Rosser's bitter disillusion when the stoppage is called off and of the shift of his political energies into self-advancement through 'dealing', though this too is persuasive. I think rather of the Glynmawr bowling green, that slow, stately, communal space where Will watches his father mowing and rolling, and Tom Rees, William Evans and the policeman John Watkins assemble in a way that manages, oddly, to be casual and ceremonious at the same time, where even political disagreements are contained within the rhythms and presence of this social space — until, that is, a quite different rhythm cuts brutally across it:

> Harry turned slowly and took Will's hand to follow. When he and the others reached the road, an Army despatch rider was passing. Watkins stood stiffly at the edge of the road: a commanding figure in the uniform stretched tightly over his huge body. A light armoured car, with an officer standing in it staring down at his map, came round the bend past the school. Behind him came eight open lorries, with about twenty steel-helmeted infantrymen in each (118).

The geographer David Harvey, whose *The Condition of Postmodernity* (1989) is another important "reassertion of space in critical social theory", argues that "working-class movements are, in fact, generally better at organizing in and dominating *place* than they are at commanding *space*" (*CP*, 236), and it is just such an insight that Williams is dramatising here. While the General Strike was indeed an instance of workers' action extending from place to space, from a single factory or industry to the totality of national economic relations, capital seems to remain one crucial, space-cancelling technological step ahead: the army's trucks versus Harry's bike, command of the wireless versus the union's telegrams. In this tense intersection of place and space, of two kinds of space and technology, the novel memorably affirms that history is fought out both within and for space, that it is precisely a 'socio-spatial dialectic'.

Finally, in the pages of *Border Country* devoted to Will's vision of the valley from above the Kestrel, on the very point of leaving it for Cambridge but not yet separated out from it, the novel does produce its utopian map, a 'pattern' which dissolves all reified 'images', and which is a decisive topographical awareness of border country. Will's gaze moves from his home valley and its farms to the Norman castles of the Lords of the March away to the east, then to the mining valleys of the south and west. History is structured by physical space, that "accident of the hidden rocks" which has laid down the coal deposits; and the interaction of these two produces distinctive kinds of social space, "blackened with pits and slag-heaps and mean grey terraces". Space, as Bachelard reminded us, "in its countless alveoli contains compressed time" (*PS*, 8); and this is certainly what space 'is for' in *Border Country* where it abruptly seems to release the very history it has shaped through and through. For "all that had been learned of the old fighting along this border stood out, suddenly, in the disposition of the castles and the roads" (*BC*, 291). "In its history the country took on a different shape", the novel tells us; but it has also shown us how to reverse this dictum and maintain — against a century of one-sided historicism — that in its shape the country takes on a different history. For *Border Country* belongs with the works of Michel Foucault, John Berger and Henri Lefebvre as a brilliant instance of Edward Soja's "precursory spatial turn" in modern cultural thought, giving vivid concrete embodiment to the theoretical insights of *Postmodern Geographies*. Only *People of the Black Mountains*, among Williams's works, rivals and indeed surpasses it in the breadth of its socio-spatial dialectic; yet space, as we shall see, remains in many different ways a fundamental structuring force in Williams's fiction.

★ ★ ★

Raymond Williams's second novel, *Second Generation* (1964), orients us towards time and history in its very title, yet it too offers rich pickings to a Bachelard-inspired topo-analysis. 'Generation' itself, surprisingly, can be understood as a spatial — and spatially baffling — phenomenon, when the 'inside' of a container also turns out to be its 'outside'. Thus Kate Owen stares, amazed, at her postgraduate son Peter: "he was so much bigger than her own tiny body that she could hardly believe he had once been a movement inside it" (*SG*, 337). And Kate's womb is related to a whole series of images of containers whose contents are secret, unexpected, dangerous: the drawer from which Myra Owen, to her daughter Beth's astonishment, takes her first husband's wedding ring; the bonnet of Gwyn Owen's car, under which his brother Harold "never wants to look . . . scared of it there like a woman" (56); the 'forbidden' inner space of Harold's own car, of which Peter makes himself the contents by stealing it; the inviolable spaces of Oxford University itself, whose secrets leave only the most fleeting traces — "the black edge of a gown disappearing, with its usual flair, into some inaccessible and confident room" (214).

Secrets inhabit enclosed spaces because, as Peter Owen declares, in the class-divided city the novel seeks to map, "the men get to confuse themselves with the buildings, that's the only trouble" (315). Williams's Oxford isn't quite Charles Dickens's London, but Peter's mother still provides a good instance of Dickens's blurring of people and buildings: strolling through Oxford with the don Arthur Dean, as their friendship as Labour Party activists approaches its adulterous consummation, she "saw its buildings with more interest and affection, as if they were extensions of her own feelings" (116). The novel may be about time, history, the generations, but then it knows full well that histories are always embodied, taking shape in rooms, buildings, spaces and settlements which in turn shape them too. *Second Generation* accordingly opens with an architectural contrast, sketching a schizophrenic "urban landscape" (its phrase) from Between Towns Road: on the one hand, the university library, with its quiet, classical, weathered dignity, and on the other the car factory where Peter's father Harold and uncle Gwyn both work:

> It is large enough to impose its own rhythms: a place of lines and regular intervals, an area rubbed clean and newly designed. It is not the huddle of mills to the course of a river, or the squat of colliery workings to the line of a seam. It needs no natural feature; it is simply a working space that has been cleared and set in order, giving room to move (10).

The space of the factory is what we might term 'Enlightenment space', a zone of pitiless productionist logic, of a 'universal' reason which has altogether abolished the local and the natural — those seams and rivers to which older technologies had to conform. As David Harvey argues of the transition from Renaissance to Enlightenment concepts of space and time: "the conquest and rational ordering of space became an integral part of the modernizing project . . . The homogenization of space poses serious difficulties for the conception of place. If the latter is the site of Being (as many theorists were later to suppose), then Becoming entails a spatial politics that renders place subservient to transformations of space" (*CP*, 249, 257). This tension between empty rationalist space and the lived intensities of place is much canvassed by the trade union activists in the novel. Should they organise their resistance around place, around local disputes in which their men will be immediately involved, or must they organise in terms of space, of the national economic framework as a whole, and risk diluting their own workers' commitment by universalist appeals to class solidarity? "It's all the one system", Rathbone militantly insists, "whatever they say about local issues, keeping local disputes separate" (107). The novel itself is more ambivalent. It deeply approves of localised struggle, as represented by Harold Owen; for, in a key place-orientated principle of the text, which challenges the various spatial fantasies of 'moving out' or 'breaking away' that it depicts, we "have to live where we are" (315). Yet on the other hand it knows all too well (as did *Border Country*) that though workers can sometimes control place, as they impressively do with the Christmas Eve march through Oxford to protest against redundancies, capital usually holds the mastery of space. The local struggles never are totalised, and if Rathbone gets his job back in West Longton, in Oxford the redundancies are eventually pushed through.

Space, then, overrides place in the factory's austere rationalism, and Williams's description of the physical rigours yet compelling abstract logic of its assembly lines is one of the best interiors or 'rooms' in his fiction:

> No hand had touched the smoothly rolling process since Harry had released the locks and Gwyn had pushed forward his controlling lever. Now, as the spit was lifted and sent back along the side of the oven, the lifting cranes were humming into position above the bodies, and the locking tackle was being fixed around them, by men who stepped in to make one practised movement and then quickly withdrew. Up went the bodies again, on to the long overhead tracks that carried them slowly round, just under the roof, to the next shop. As Gwyn reversed his lever, the forks and the turntable moved slowly back into position. Already, from the vibrant heat of the oven, a new spit was poised to emerge, with its identical russet bodies (87).

It seems entirely appropriate that the product here is the motor-car, which threatens the 'spatialising' of place across the whole society. As in *Border Country*, technologies of transport are read as indices of deep social commitments. Peter Owen characteristically walks, "haunting the street with that sort of accusing walk" as his ex-girlfriend Rose Swinburne puts it. If this walk is itself a kind of obsessive enclosure, its utopian counterpart is given by a tiny physical adjustment of May Lane's, out Christmas shopping with her husband Robert: "it seemed very simple, just stepping from the pavement" (255), and this single pace, which takes her into the car-workers' demonstration, could be seen as a direct challenge to Matthew Price's self-protective shift into empty space in Gwenton station. If Peter walks, Rose cycles, Kate takes the bus, and Arthur Dean drives. Cycling, between Williams's two first novels, has passed decisively over from place to space. It once denoted Harry Price's dogged rootedness as against Morgan Rosser's dubious mobility, but now signals all that was evoked in *Border Country* by the term 'image'. In Rose's case, it denotes the conscious projection of a style for consumption by others, a facade with no underlying substance, a mobile sophisticated consciousness mimicking the accoutrements of place for the sake of a quaint, primitivistic thrill; her cycling is exactly this, as is that gentrified "terrace of nineteenth-century cottages, originally built by a college for the families of its servants" where she lives (154). "England is still the museum", declares Helen Edwards at an Oxford sherry party (315); and Rose is constructing her life *as* museum, turning actual history into a stylish pastiche of itself — a general cultural phenomenon that will preoccupy Williams intensely in *The Volunteers* with its Welsh Folk Museum.

Buses, in *Border Country*, were already ambivalent: Matthew senses the socio-spatial implications of their physical construction (those isolating high-backed seats), but had also experienced a kind of epiphany of community, a "sudden closeness of contact", aboard one on the way to Gwenton (*BC*, 314). In *Second Generation* they still have a vaguely approving aura, hinting in a ghostly way at the value of public provision rather than private consumerism; but they have now been decisively caught up in alien spatial rhythms. Travelling into Oxford to meet Arthur, Kate sees pedestrians transformed by the very rhythm of her motion into the ghoulish sub-human city dwellers of T.S. Eliot's *The Waste Land*, into 'masses', that contemptuous hegemonic way of seeing that so much of Williams's early social writing sets out to defeat; for "it was difficult, in the brief moment as the bus passed, to see them as real" (126). The love of Arthur and Kate is governed by the car from the start, getting under way through lifts back after Labour Party meetings; and this, in the novel's view, is enough to damn it, quite apart from its extra-marital nature.

But if *Second Generation* still knows where its Morgan Rossers are, it is much less confident that it can find a Harry Price to pit against them. What Raymond Williams in later years termed 'mobile privatisation', of which the car is one notable instance, seems to have soaked through the entire society; the novel's Oxford is a city of relentless traffic rather than dreaming spires, a "highway to which everything comes, the shuttle and tension of all the other actions" (10). "What was central now was the fact of traffic", the book tells us (234), and many of its most energetic scenes are of traffic movements, large- or small-scale: Peter driving alone in the Welsh mountains and tempted by suicide with a single wrench of the steering wheel, or the great tide of traffic that leaves the works at clocking-off time. The political highlight of the book then logically turns out to be a moment of 'anti-traffic', that Christmas Eve protest march which the police want to dissuade precisely because it might "finish the traffic off for good" (194). (One further, related transport technology which constitutes a minor obsession in Williams's fiction in its own right is the motorbike, which kills Jack Evans in *Second Generation*, constantly threatens to kill Trevor Jenkins in *The Fight for Manod*, and does kill Georgi in *Loyalties*; this is perhaps in all his work the one 'border' (between car and bike) that Williams will have no truck with).

The central socio-spatial reality of *Second Generation* is this rush and shuttling of traffic through Enlightenment space, a 'post-natural' space which offers no resistance or obstruction. The novel speaks of the "clear *functional* shape of the factory buildings" (12, emphasis added), and its adjective links the car works back to the great buildings of early twentieth-century architecture. For the modernist artefacts of Le Corbusier, Walter Gropius and Mies van der Rohe — gleaming white, rectilinear, flat-roofed, thoroughly streamlined — were indeed rigorously functionalist, stripped bare of all ornament and making no concessions at all to personal taste or local context. Architectural modernism, the so-called International Style, rejects *Second Generation's* insistence that "we have to live where we are". It spurns the local, that degraded city-fabric around its dazzling white self, rejecting all historical styles and traditions, and offers to make a completely new start, based on a strict logic of state-of-the-art building materials and techniques or on the impersonal function of the building. Modernist architecture, we can say, is the appropriate type of building for Enlightenment space; both reject local traditions — what they see as mere 'prejudices' or 'superstitions' — in favour of an appeal to pure reason. This mode of architectural modernism, just hinted at here in the car factory, will expand to become a major preoccupation of Williams's fourth novel *The Fight for Manod*.

"There is a fence around the works", *Second Generation* notes, "but the rhythms cross it, into the first line of houses" (12); and they do not stop there, by any means. Functionalist space and its traffic transforms many of the rooms, homes and buildings of this novel, gutting the interior of Rose's cottage into a space as bleakly abstract as that of the factory itself: "sparsely furnished, in Rose's deliberate style . . . 'I mean it's living-space, primarily,' was all she would say. There was indeed hardly any pressure of objects, defining a way to live" (154). Such spaces, in conformity with the socio-spatial dialectic, then programme the very sexual encounters (Rose and Peter) that take place within them, reducing human love-making to their own desiccation. Not that "pressure of objects", in its own right, is any guarantee that you have escaped Enlightenment space. Le Corbusier notoriously defined a house as "a machine for living in", and the kitchen of Peter's supervisor, Robert Lane, comes impressively close to being this: "like a gleaming workshop, with the quiet hum of machinery: the throb of the refrigerator, the deeper and harsher beat of the oil central heating . . . the white enamel of the fitted sink and electric mixer" (73). The very clutter of gadgetry by which Lane, on this miniature scale, seeks to turn space into place in fact only further confirms the alienation of the latter in the former.

From the beginning, the novel asks what kind of feasible human habitation, what kind of *place*, could we imagine, desire and struggle for in this space-ridden culture. Whereas the room-which-was-not-a-room in *Border Country* was a relatively minor textual detail, *Second Generation* aggressively confronts us with such an unsettling non-room from the very start, a "room to be constructed" which is the measure of the spatial challenge which awaits us:

> He saw his reflection ahead of him, in the bright window of a furniture store. The curved and bevelled mirrors, hung at varying heights, were reflecting the light in a multitude of angles . . . There was a lattice of red-printed stickers on the long window, repeating again and again *Bedroom Event*. Behind the wide plate glass . . . a pink-quilted bed rested between the mirrored pieces of a veneered suite of two wardrobes and a dressing-table. Curly pink-shaded lamps mixed into the grey of the autumn evening (11).

This is a room which the novel can hardly name as such, a room whose component units are all present but which conveys no sense of a living totality, and whose only possible unity, surely, is as the space of 'fantasy' (a key term in this book), of those forbidden 'bedroom events' to which so much of this novel is indeed devoted. Mirrors and rooms, as here, interact in strange ways; and much later, as Arthur confronts Kate once their affair has become public knowledge, he notices how "her long hair brushed the convex mirror in which the room was distortedly reflected" (272). Rather as with the non-room off the living room in *Border Country*, mirrors seem helpfully to supplement or duplicate the space of a room, but in so doing strangely hollow it out, making of actually occupied space a fluid, indeterminate zone open to all kinds of unconscious investment. Something similar may be said of the wardrobes here. "Does there", Gaston Bachelard asks, "exist a single dreamer of words who does not respond to the word wardrobe?"; and we can describe Raymond Williams too, in Bachelard's phrase, as being in a minor way a "poet of furniture" (*PS*, 78). The wardrobe, Bachelard tells us, is an "entity of depth", and might we therefore be justified in seeing Harry Price's sombre mahogany wardrobe as in a sense containing all the flashback sequences which constitute the body of the novel, just as the wardrobes of *Second Generation* announce secrets to be unconcealed?

The mother's body, as we have seen, is an empty room/womb because its son has left it, and the son senses her aching emptiness. The dark kitchen to which he walks home in the opening pages is an early sign of how much is wrong with his family (in contrast to the "curtain of warm air and the smell of cooking" which characterises his uncle and aunt's home, 14); and when he later tries to visualise his mother, "he could see only a dark room, a long room where there might have been a meeting" (31). The dire social paradox of *Second Generation* is that the wearing struggle against capitalism so drains its working-class opponents (here Harold and Kate Owen) that they come in a sense to resemble it, bled dry of warm human substance and as contemptuous of the consumerist 'apathy' of their fellow-workers as is the system itself. But where previous commentators have traced this paradox through as a human process, I want to map it as, again, a spatial one, though these are not in the long run separable issues. If Enlightenment space reaches out from the factory to desiccate the lived space of the politically active workers, then how might it be challenged? What kind of humane space — room or habitat, a place rather than a space — is still feasible under the centrifugal pressures of unrelenting traffic? The novel has two answers to this conundrum, the 'shell' and the 'nest', though as I shall show it can finally settle for neither.

The intense need to inhabit, despite the wastes of abstract space sweeping across and through one, is suggested throughout the novel by unconscious bodily rhythms and movements. In our first extended glimpse of Kate she is "lying with her arms folded around her breasts, and her fingers were tight on her shoulders, pulling in to herself for comfort and warmth" (38). The body aims to reduce or even annihilate itself, to become a protective enclosure *for* itself, its own nest, or to become so diminutive (Kate is physically very small in the first place) that the rhythms of traffic will simply overlook and pass it by. This initial gesture of Kate's then becomes compulsive. She "sat back deeply, with her legs curled under her", "her hands . . . tightly clasped over her ankles", "curled in the big chair" (51–2); or, in a socio-spatial pun, curling can become coiling as its pain and need increase till "her whole body was coiled tight and trembling" (54). And if there is one word that gets Gaston Bachelard's adrenalin running even faster than "wardrobe" does, it is, precisely, to curl: "in our houses we have nooks and corners in which we like to curl up comfortably. To curl up belongs to the phenomenology of the verb to inhabit, and only those who have learned to do so can inhabit with intensity" (*PS*, xxxiv).

One could hardly "curl up" in Lane's gadget-cluttered kitchen or Rose's empty rooms, so the novel's first locus of curling, coiling and clinging is, as the furniture store had already announced, the bed. Our first view of Kate is of her lying in bed reading and "slipping down" further and further into it; and sex with Arthur Dean, which she later admits never amounted to all that much, is perhaps a pretext for re-experiencing the 'bed-ness' of beds rather than a real passion in its own right. Once the affair gets under way in earnest, Kate creates a mirage or simulacrum of a room at home, as formally perfect at all points as the room in the furniture store but a space in which, like the tiny non-room in *Border Country*, nothing human can any longer happen; the very diligence that goes into the preparation of its surfaces and details over-compensates for the inner 'curling-ness' which it now lacks. The room becomes, in effect, a museum to the marriage whose living territory it once was, and Kate enters the one-dimensional spatial world of Rose Swinburne, converting living history into glossy waxwork. The effect of this simulacrum of a kitchen is to drive her husband Harold back to *his* bed, the last nook where he can still curl and nestle.

Whereas initially Kate's was the immobile body, reading magazines in bed while Harold busily deals with trade-union affairs at the factory, this spatial power relation is more and more reversed as the novel proceeds, so that our characteristic view of the pair is Harold huddled in his bed, "unshaven, and without his teeth" (286), while his wife perches on its edge with a cup of tea, eager to head off to organise a march, attend a political meeting or make love to Arthur.

However, though you can certainly curl up in an actual, empirical bed, beds don't satisfy that Bachelardian craving for a more radical kind of curling, an ontologically deep kind of inhabiting. *Second Generation* is a novel much concerned with fantasy, of which it usually disapproves, recommending instead the dour necessity to "live where we are", to spend yet another summer holiday in a wet Welsh caravan rather than jet off for once to Paris, as Kate desires. Yet the novel's ire is directed only at the "fantasy of the personal break-out, through sex" or otherwise (272), fantasies of speed and escape which simply internalise the very rhythms of the culture they were supposed to liberate you from. For *Second Generation* has its own fantasies, of habitation rather than break-out, of spaces more charged, more violently 'curl-able' than any actual bed, nook or cranny you could ever find. Some of these fantasies, I admit, are nightmarish rather than utopian, charged with horror rather than desire, or desire which, repressed, has turned to horror. These fantasies then demand a psychoanalytical interpretation, as we should expect of a novel in which Robert Lane tosses technical analytic terms like 'projection' and 'displacement' into his every conversation. The central space of horror in this text bursts into consciousness when Peter Owen finally discovers the missing human contents of the simulated room in the furniture store, when its "plate-glass" of repression shatters and the sinister "curling" of its Bedroom Events is blazoned forth: "Peter was standing in the doorway, quite still. Unconsciously, Harold slackened the pull of his hands. Kate brought her head forward" (209). This is a scene of violence rather than sex, but then, as Freud insisted, the child invariably (mis)understands its parents' lovemaking as a physical attack by the father on the mother. With the father's denunciations of his adulterous wife — "you're filth . . . Filth all through" — still ringing in his ears, Peter stumbles traumatically upon a Freudian primal scene, a space of paternal sexual violence and the betrayal and soiling of a mother who lets the father use her body rather than preserving it intact for her son. Faced with so severe a "return of the repressed", Peter flees desperately, achieving what minor Oedipal retaliation he can by stealing his father's car and violating its sealed space. Even much later, as the Owens move toward reconciliation, the father still has a striking ability to inflict spatial metamorphosis and disaster on his son; no sooner does Harold visit Peter in his new bedsit than we witness "a bareness and shabbiness in the room that Peter hadn't previously noticed" (329).

There are spaces of Enlightenment reason, in which even secret cavities have been deprived of mystery by functionalism, as with Myra and her ilk "looking into the bag to make to sure all their functions were there: purse, shopping list, key, compact and mirror" (39); and psychoanalytical spaces whose mysteries terrify. But where shall we find a space that is charged with both mystery and pleasure, the solace of curling? The novel's answer is: in the shell or nest, which have incorporated the very rhythm of curling in the structure of their organic curvilinear architecture. The shell in *Second Generation* is Uncle Gwyn's conservatory, a "lightened shell" with "a different quality in it, both of humidity and of the smell of growth":

> The glass was misted, and with the light inside it the whole structure seemed of a different substance from the things we ordinarily look at. The neat staging and shelves were lined with pots, which threw sharp angled shadows down on the glass. But around these, seen through the misting, were the intricate networks of the growing plants, and the occasional flash of colour where the light reflected the flowers (14).

This, clearly, is magical space, a space of childhood as enticing as Will Price's flap-table. It is also a space of magical light, whose only challenger in this respect is the glimpses of college towers which punctuate the narrative, "the floodlit tower, where the beautiful stonework seemed transformed into solid light" (114). Attractive such glimpses may be, but the colleges remain an architecture of power and exclusion, and what is so compelling about the conservatory is that its "different substance" allows light to shine through and not just on it; it becomes a crystal lit from within rather than illuminated from without. The theme of the organic is important here, as it is later when Peter digs for leaf-mould with his uncle in High Wood; but the point about this "lighted shell" is its organic hardness, as a casing within which animal or plant life protectedly dwells. For the question of how 'hard' one should be, politically and otherwise, absorbs *Second Generation*. It is certainly possible to be too 'soft', and images of wet, mushy squelchiness just passing over from the attractive to the disgusting are prevalent in Williams's fiction: the "pear so yellow and soft that his fingers mushed in it as he held" in *Border Country* (35), the guavas that Norman and Emma Braose eat "slowly, enjoying their softness" and then invoke as social metaphor in *Loyalties* (126), or Kate's desperate kiss in *Second Generation* — "her lips were wet and moving, and seemed to be drawing him into her" (110). But it is no less possible, and indeed far more likely, to be too 'hard', either through the sexual promiscuity that Beth denounces ("aren't really like women, once they've hardened", 20) or in the grim human cost of political activism according to Kate; "we've exposed ourselves and we've hardened" (340). The translucent shell offers an ideal resolution to this dilemma: it is mineral or crystalline enough to protect the soft vegetable processes it contains, yet not so hard that it altogether obscures that inner life or 'curling' behind armourplating.

If Peter dreams of shells, his mother hankers after nests, a form of habitation for which she seems to be preparing her body throughout the novel. Constantly making her tiny body more tiny, she, like Gaston Bachelard, "returns to images that, in order for us to live in them, require us to become very small, as in nests and shells" (*PS*, xxxiv). If I suggest that her fascination with the activity of birds during her final walk with Peter — "several birds in the bare thorn hedge, and she looked at them with sudden interest" (336) — is an effort to digest, on the spot, something of the mechanics of nest-building, the reader will doubtless conclude that I am being fanciful. But then *Second Generation* too is devoted to fantasy, to outlining utopian fantasies of habitation as well as unmasking spatial fantasies of "break-out". For what, even to a topo-analyst, remains the most remarkable thing about this novel is the fact that it does indeed contain a real human nest, one inhabited by Arthur Dean's uncle:

> In his last years in Cornwall he started a rite of spring . . . On the
> first of March every year he had a nest built in his bedroom. A
> substantial thing of interwoven hazel branches, lined with straw
> and moss. Then for the next six weeks he lived in the nest. A
> servant he'd brought back used to take up his food, and he ate and
> slept there, everything . . . the nest got pretty foul, but only he
> had to put up with it (114–5).

This is, perhaps, the most bizarre passage in all of Raymond
Williams's fiction, though, as we shall see, it has many echoes and
analogues in the later novels. In *The Poetics of Space* Gaston
Bachelard proposes the grand task of a "philosophical
phenomenology of nests" and the more modest one of a "search for
nests in literature"; and had he happened upon *Second Generation*,
he would have found an instance better than many of those he cites.
The prowess of birds as inhabitants had already featured in *Border
Country*, where a flock of homing pigeons is released just as Will
takes the train to Cambridge, implicitly guaranteeing his own
eventual return. "Bird architecture", Bachelard maintains, is "a
house built by and for the body, taking form from the inside", from
the continual pressing of the female bird's breast whereby it
smooths and curves its rough materials (*PS*, 101). More than any
other mode of architecture, it bears the lived impress of the body,
and this makes it a powerful counter-assertion to the inhuman
abstractions of the International Style and its industrial
counterparts.

Moreover, the nest is a neat compromise between the
habitational fantasies of Kate Owen and Arthur Dean. Perched at
the top of a tree, it satisfies his desire for aerial remoteness ("we
don't normally see roofs enough", he tells Kate, 50); but, since it is
made of earth and one can huddle deeply into it, the nest also
satisfies Kate's longing for some burrow that plunges into the
depths — for which hands thrust to the bottom of pockets or body
withdrawn ever deeper into beds and armchairs are her feeble
substitutes elsewhere in the novel. Robert Lane describes Arthur
and Kate's relationship as an "interlocking of fantasies" (265), and
in this matter of the nest his phrase is exactly apt. And there may
well be, lurking in the textual background here, a traditional
literary pun on cuckold/cuckoo, with Harold as the former and
Arthur the latter, laying his amorous eggs in the nests of others.

In this strange passage, then, the novel gives spatial substance to what has previously been just hint, nuance or metaphor, and it does so, interestingly, in the context of race and Empire. Arthur's nesting uncle had made his money in rubber in Malaya and fathered a child by a Chinese girl he kept as his mistress. It is then notable how often moments of imaginative or sexual excitement in Williams's fiction are bound up with racial otherness. The moment Matthew Price began running, revelling in his own physical activity, he meets a black woman; and in *Second Generation* the moment Peter and Beth start dancing, recovering a physical ease with each other that they've lost through the tension of Peter's years at university, they meet the African nationalists at an Oxford party. Indeed, the meeting with the Africans is sandwiched between this renewed physicality and Peter and Beth's first full sexual experience together. At a level well below the novel's official political discourse here, which has Peter and the Africans agreeing that one has to live "where one is", the Africans are an integral part of that love-making. A fantasy of racial otherness obscurely inhabits it, just as it does that startling appearance of a gigantic human nest in a novel many critics have complained of as dully realist.

If the tiny room in the Prices' cottage was a room-which-is-not-a-room, the nest in *Second Generation* is a room which is more than a room, a hyper-room or room raised to the second power, tensely curling in upon itself to ward off that tremendous acceleration of traffic, of swift monads tearing through abstract unresisting space, that threatens in this novel to tear all walls down and to make place into either pure space or a mere museum of itself. The structuring spatial opposition here is, clearly, nest versus traffic, lived enclosure versus vertiginous mobility; and traffic is winning. With their odd supplementary spaces, rooms were already unstable in *Border Country*, and they are much more so in its successor. The part of them which seems most secure in *Second Generation* and where, accordingly, much of its action takes place is, oddly enough, the very spot where they cease to be, their doors. The novel opens in Between Towns Road, but continues in a Between Rooms Space, in doorways, which seem to obsess it. Or perhaps we should say that the doorway is a tense compromise between rooms and traffic, which the novel accordingly clings to or curls round: guaranteeing

Pandy School, Raymond Williams front row, far left.

Abergavenny Grammar School First XV, 1937-38
Raymond Williams standing, second right

Editor of the *Cambridge University Journal*, 1941

Williams the grammar school boy, outside the family home in Pandy, c. 1938

Call-up photograph, Royal Corps of Signals,
Prestatyn, 1941

Service overseas with the 21st Anti-Tank Regiment

Outside Pandy signal box during the making of the film *The Country, the City*

Reading from *Second Generation* at a launch in Cardiff

'The Ship' earthworks, Hateral Ridge, the Black Mountains, which appear as 'Banavint' in People of the Black Mountains. Photograph by Raymond Williams

'The Black Darren', the Black Mountains. Photograph by Raymond Williams.

On a family walk in the Black Mountains

"Third Generational": at Pandy with grandson Bryn

Raymond Williams after climbing 'The Cat's Back' in the Black Mountains

mobility and egress, it is the point where, spatially speaking, a room metamorphoses into speed or traffic without entirely ceasing to be itself. If *Border Country* sought to make rooms 'room-y', *Second Generation* just as vividly makes doors 'door-y', alerting us to the ways they both reflect and structure social relations.

Its most extended image of this, the equivalent in terms of doors of Arthur's uncle's nest, occurs in Rose's house. The key conversation between her and Peter, which ends in their going to bed together, occurs while she is painting the sitting-room door, an act of painting which, as any reader can testify, goes on and on and on:

> Peter stood looking at the sitting-room door, where the paint was wet and half-finished.
> 'Are you going to finish it?' he asked.
> 'Sure.' . . .
> He took off his jacket, and sat back. At the open door, Rose was sitting with her legs apart and the pot of paint between her ankles, leaning forward and painting one of the lower panels (165).

In its thematic context, the door is an apt locale, since Peter and Rose discuss the extent to which sex is either private or public; the door, as a boundary between domestic and public space, illustrates the point. But the obsessive painting sprawls on until it is the 'doorness' of the door that preoccupies us, not its role as metaphor in an argument. For it is not just a line or marker between spaces, but a profoundly active space in its own right. It is, for instance, a decisive zone of sexuality; the barely registered sexual attraction prompted by Rose's posture at the door, "with her legs apart", will later impel them upstairs together. Throughout this novel doors seem to structure sexuality, for it is in doorways, at the entrances to rooms, that women in *Second Generation* seem always likely to expose the entrances to their bodies. A notable instance is Kate getting out of Harold's car on the wrong side: "as she reached the door he saw that her skirt had ridden back up her legs" (191), and it is no accident that later, as he waits in the secretary's office at the car works, Harold "watched the swing of her skirt as she went through the door" (281). The sexuality of the door may be conscious rather than unconscious, sought-out rather than fortuitous, when the door is no longer a neutral marker between public and private but a space of eager and furtive erotic privacy in its own right, as when "a few couples had moved back into the darkness of the doorways" (234).

A semiotics of doors was already at work in *Border Country*: the back door of a cottage is a site of intimacy, easy access and neighbourliness, while its front door signifies ceremony, officialdom and ultimately death; for at his father's funeral "Matthew stood shaking hands with every one who arrived. This morning nobody went to the back door" (*BC*, 342). And I cited earlier the passage on great men, cupboards and doorkeepers by which Matthew evokes the socio-spatial deadness of England. Doors remain intermittently important throughout Williams's fiction, and my own favourite would be the Ministerial door in *The Fight for Manod*, which in its own physical structure incarnates the suave gentlemanly urbanity with which raw power in this society is mediated and muted. Peter Owen "tried to slam it behind him but it moved so slowly, on its heavy springs, that it did not even quite close" (*FM*, 193). But their strange because liminal spaces, tiny border countries in their own right, are most fully mapped in *Second Generation*. Doors turn out to be places of great power, either sexual (as in the voyeuristic moments I've already noted) or social or both, since the doorkeepers of the powerful are usually female: the girl Glynis who bars Matthew from Dr Evans's surgery in *Border Country*, the secretary who hesitates whether she should open the boss's door for Harold as union representative in *Second Generation*. A key moment of danger in a relationship, repeatedly in the latter novel, occurs when someone determinedly occupies a doorway, as does Harold after intercepting his wife at Arthur Dean's flat ("He did not answer, but stood blocking the door", 206), or Peter when he menaces old Wyndham Evans in the petrol station at Trawsfynydd.

But if you can block doors, doors can also block you, having acquired some stubborn, silent power of resistance which makes them virtually walls in their own right. At the novel's opening Peter is turned back by the door of the side passage to his house, and at its close Kate is rebuffed by the gate to High Wood, for "at the gate leading into it they instinctively stopped" (338). Zones of power and intimidation, doors are also, for the intimidated, sites of refuge and security; even if there is no actual intention to escape, they at least faintly announce its formal possibility. When Rose's sexual taunts seem "overwhelmingly stronger than his sense of himself" Peter "put out his hand to the edge of the door, and held on to it tightly" (184); in a difficult encounter with Peter, Beth "was holding the outside edge of the door. He looked at the line of her hand and wrist" (237); and when Arthur turns up in her home, Kate "was afraid to move, or even to let go of the handle she was holding" (269). It is in such tiny details that we can measure the distance between Raymond Williams's first two novels, for there was a "poetry of handles" in *Border Country* too when, for example, after his father's death, in the shed Matthew "impulsively . . . reached for the handle" of the hacker and "let his fingers close round the smooth wood . . . find a strange reassurance" (*BC*, 324) — a reassurance echoed years later in *Loyalties*, where a pick handle becomes a political legacy in its own right. The hand that lovingly labours in a known place gives way in *Second Generation* to the hand adrift in a space which has few bearings, a hand clutching a door handle domineeringly or in terror but always provisionally, always about to let go and move on.

Hands, indeed, are what *Second Generation* is in the end all about. Characters in the novel talk incessantly about the dangers of being 'broken', to the point where — however genuine the economic, political or sexual pressures are — the term itself becomes infuriating or even risible in its repetitions. Yet in an alarmingly literal sense human bodies *are* broken in the text, reified into autonomous organs which no longer recognise each other as kin. Such fragmentation, as we might expect, is the effect of power: "The white-sleeved arms came over the gowned shoulders with ease and regularity. In the rush of talk, there was not time to look up and see where the arms came from" (258). Part-objects with a detached will of their own, the arms that were once college servants correspond to the "hands" that the car-workers and even their bosses have become; and the novel's most impassioned political plea, articulated by Kate, is for a new imagination of the whole body. Reflecting on the redundancy notices, she cries: "No man could write 'parts of the labour force'. Wouldn't he look, while he was writing it, at his own hand, at himself?" (190). But the shift from part to whole, from hand to "himself", is not so easily made. Even in the more integrated world of *Border Country* there was a strange bodily disjunction in Harry Price who seems,

Frankenstein-like, to have been cobbled together out of the spare parts of several different corpses; for "the solidity of the face and body made the extreme smallness of the hands and feet sudden and surprising" (*BC*, 27). In *Second Generation* the divorce between part-object and total body widens: pairs of hands scrabble around the wastes of Enlightenment space searching for bodies to belong to. A series of reductive metamorphoses afflict any full bodies the novel strives to depict: "Robert now he remembered: the hands spread on the rail of the bridge of the meadow" (313); Harold shrinks down to "the hands that had torn at the hair, forcing the head back and down. The darkness in the hands" (215); even Peter, driving through Wales, dwindles to a "decision wholly localised now, in the light touch of his hands" (221). Kate too seems to be assailed by this alarming autonomisation of hands, plunging hers as deep as they'll go in her pockets as if to keep some vestige of control over them; and a fascination with hands as entities in their own right comes through even in Williams's critical writings in an extended, and in context baffling, contrast of his own hands, "covered with hair", with those of F.R. Leavis, "the backs were quite smooth" (*WICS*, 22).

But if the body is so pulverised, broken into a scattered jigsaw of its former self, then its fantasies of dwelling will shrink down to this level too. The nest of Arthur's uncle is in the end an amazing exception, and as so many of the characters in *Second Generation* tell us at one point or another, the "margin is narrow". What this means, spatially, is that fantasies of curling, of marking out a place against the rigours of space, speed and traffic, are only achievable at the level of the fragmented hand. It is in the end, *pace* Bachelard, not the total body which is made so tiny that it might clamber into a nest or shell, as all the rest of that body which is chopped away so that the hand alone can curl round or cup that nest, thereby — in Bachelard's terms — "expressing the function of inhabiting in terms of touch" (*PS*, 131). The Owens do finally settle their conflicts, with Kate and Harold coming together sexually again, Peter and Beth announcing impending marriage, and Peter resuming his intellectual work. And yet the political ambitions of the novel, which once took the form of Arthur Dean's "absolute demand" against capitalist inhumanity, have diminished to what Gaston Bachelard calls a "phenomenology of roundness . . . a sort of intimacy of roundness", a recreation of the nest within the hand: "images of *full roundness* help us to collect ourselves, to confer an initial constitution on ourselves, and to confirm our being intimately, inside" (*PS*, 234).

Good space in *Second Generation*, under the pressure of so many kinds of inhumane space, shrinks to a series of pleasurable roundnesses held in the hand, topophilia on the smallest possible human scale: Gwyn — "cupped now in his left hand was a ball of black fibre" (23); Kate — "crumpled the paper again . . . It was as if she could feel his hand in the rough ball of paper" (39); Peter — "moving his hands inside her jersey and touching her breasts with his fingers" (184); Arthur Dean — "moving his hands affectionately around his wine glass" (262); Peter again, on the scaffolding — "tracing its structure as if in his hands . . . feeling the hold of the fingers on the long bars" (335). The only "dwelling" that can be communally built is a set of hands cradling wine glasses, as Harold, Kate, Gwyn and Myra toast Peter and Beth. In a brilliant spatial pun, Williams makes the wine they select "a French wine, Hermitage, from the Rhone valley" (343). "Catch you in a hermitage", Harold at once retorts to Kate, pointing up the fantasy of habitation that is at work here. In one direction, through the association with hermit crabs, we recall the desirable "lighted shell" that was Gwyn's conservatory. In another direction and if we have read *The Poetics of Space*, we recall Bachelard on the space of the hermit. The hermit's hut, he argues, derives its truth "from the intensity of its essence, which is the essence of the verb 'to inhabit' ": "the hut appears to be the tap-root of the function of inhabiting" (*PS*, 31–32). To its very last breath, then, its last gasp of spatial and linguistic ingenuity, *Second Generation* strives to keep alive the memory of the good place, of the utopian spaces of the nest, in a culture of sheer speed and empty, rationalised space which leaves such memories ever fewer nooks and chinks to curl and cling to.

3

From Realism to Postmodernism: *The Fight for Manod* and *The Volunteers*

S
econd Generation was published in 1964, four years after *Border Country*, and the relationship between the two novels is very close indeed. For there is a sense in which *Second Generation* actually belongs within *Border Country*, giving us as it does the experience of the working-class student (Peter Owen) at an ancient university which was the 'missing' core of the first novel. But Raymond Williams's next two novels, *The Volunteers* and *The Fight for Manod*, were published after a hiatus of some fourteen years, in 1978 and 1979 respectively, and differ markedly in form from their predecessors. In terms of simple bulk, both together add up to the length of only one of the first two novels. Narratively, they frustrate by their very brevity; so effective are they, we want there to be more, whereas *Border Country* and *Second Generation* were leisurely and spacious in their telling, even to the point of occasional *longueur*. This is not just a matter of cuts forced upon their author by tight-fisted editors, though he sometimes explained it in such terms. *The Volunteers* is the simple case: its compression and pace result from a decisive formal break in Williams's fictional career, from the realist novel to political thriller as its hero, Lewis Redfern, tracks down the terrorist group which has shot a Government Minister. *The Fight for Manod* is more difficult, since despite the hiatus it features both Matthew Price and Peter Owen, working together as consultants for a government plan to build a new city from scratch in a mid-Wales valley, and offers to be the completion of what has come to be known as Williams's 'Welsh trilogy'. *Manod* proves tricky to classify generically since, as I shall argue below, it contains notable elements of detective fiction, apocalypse, Gothic horror story and

even science-fiction, but also, in its patient, detailed exploration of the working lives of farming families in the Afren valley, clearly extends the realist impulse of Williams's earlier fiction. *The Fight for Manod* is, I suggest, a realist 'limit-text', a work where literary realism stumbles upon something which exceeds its grasp, falters badly, but is not altogether quelled. And I shall aim to relate this sense of generic limits, tensions and fissures to the new social reality which *Manod* and *The Volunteers* so persuasively portray, what Robert Lane in the former calls "the new drift, the new indifference, brittleness of this stage of capitalism", a "system so shifting, so complex" as to defeat the realist text entirely (*FM*, 16, 18).

The issue of realism is a crucial one in any discussion of Raymond Williams's fiction. His chapter on 'Realism and the Contemporary Novel' in *The Long Revolution* in 1961 ends with the declaration that "a new realism is necessary, if we are to remain creative" (316); fifteen years later, in 1976, he gave a lecture to a *Screen* weekend school entitled 'A Defence of Realism', and in *Politics and Letters* in 1979 he was still speculating on "the future of a new realism" (*PL*, 224). The 1961 essay claims to offer "a possible new meaning of realism" (*LR*, 300), but we can see now, as Williams could not at the time, how close his version of realism is to that of Georg Lukács, particularly in the latter's classic essay, 'Narrate or Describe?' (1936). Later, as Lukács's works were translated, Williams readily acknowledged kinship: "I feel very close in approach to Lukács over the realist novel" (*PL*, 349), and I shall invoke Lukács on realism in addition to Williams to shed light on the interplay of time and space in the classical realist novel.

The core of Raymond Williams's early definition of realism is swiftly given. "When I think of the realist tradition in fiction, I think of the kind of novel which creates and judges the quality of a whole way of life in terms of the qualities of persons" (*LR*, 304). He is led to this view by a sense of a "formal gap in modern fiction", a gap which he traces back historically to the splitting apart of the "balance" of the realist form at the end of the nineteenth century. Whereas George Eliot and Leo Tolstoy saw both the general society and their individual characters as interactive elements of a "whole indivisible process" (306), the novel after them falls apart into 'social' and 'personal' modes, each of which then again divides into 'documentary' and 'formula' sub-modes. What interests me here is a preliminary moment within the split, with realism mutating into something else but not yet having fully becoming the 'social documentary' novel which for Williams is the end-point of this mutation. He does not give a name to this moment, though with Lukács's work in mind we would probably now call it Naturalism; it appears, around the century, in "writers like Bennett". The true realist vision, Williams contends:

> is not realized by detailed stocktaking descriptions of shops or back-parlours or station waiting rooms. These may be used, as elements of the action, but they are not this essential realism. If they are put in, for the sake of description as such, they may in fact destroy the balance that is the essence of this method; they may, for example, transfer attention from the people to the things. It was actually this very feeling, that in this kind of fully-furnished novel everything was present but actual individual life, that led, in the 1920s, to the disrepute of realism (*LR*, 305–6).

In view of the immense attention to rooms and spaces, to containers and their contents, in *Border Country* and *Second Generation* these formulations are already surprising. But they are certainly entirely Lukácsian. Williams's contrast between 'action' and mere 'description' corresponds exactly to Lukács's stark choice — narrate *or* describe; and for Lukács too description is a matter of space: "One describes what one sees, and the spatial 'present' confers a temporal 'present' on men and objects. But it is an illusory present, not the present of immediate action of the drama" (*WC*, 130). For both critics, this false realism involves spatial 'reification': spaces, rooms, objects within them, determine the human characters, rather than vice versa. 'True' realism, on the other hand, is devoted to time, history, the active human will; it shows rooms and objects *being* made, as determined not determining. Classical realism, then, to return to Edward Soja's terms in *Postmodern Geographies*, is a 'historicism'; it believes that the context of time, history, change and narration is always and everywhere the most relevant framework for interpreting human behaviour; this is fully explicit in Lukács, and I believe implicit in Raymond Williams's formulations. Though both critics pay lip-service to the 'balance' or 'interaction' of space and time in realism, since what human beings make in turn makes them, in practice they always emphasise time over space. Naturalist description, which aims to show space as actively formative rather than passively being formed, thus comes in for heavy attack from them; as ever, historicism can only see space as — to return to Michel Foucault's epithets — the dead, the fixed, the undialectical, or the immobile. Both Williams and Lukács agree that there has been a disastrous split in the realist tradition, but they periodise this differently. For Lukács, the key date is 1848. Before this, history can be seen in its active, revolutionary making, and the writer was not a closeted professional but a lively participant in that process; after the defeat of the 1848 revolutions, the possibilities of change vanish, history is now product not process, the novelist retreats into his study, and narration succumbs to description. Raymond Williams, in both *The Long Revolution* and *The English Novel*, locates realism's "period of crisis and of a parting of the ways" much later in the century, around the 1890s, in what we would now call the "age of imperialism" (*EN*, 119); and his observations on this crisis of realism or narration dovetail with the recent three stage history of space worked out by Fredric Jameson in his project for a "spatial analysis of culture" ('CM', 348). I want to use Jameson's spatial literary history as a way of suggesting that even *Border Country* and *Second Generation*, admirable realist novels which do indeed live up to the terms of Williams's 1961 definition, also display an uneasy subterranean knowledge that in the baffling new world of the mid-twentieth century realism may no longer be able to perform the cultural mission assigned to it.

Most novels, Williams writes in *The English Novel*, are "knowable communities", and in his history of the novel from Dickens to Lawrence and beyond, he takes "one bearing as central: the exploration of community: the substance and meaning of community" (*EN*, 11). But a knowable community depends on a certain kind of social space, one compact and coherent enough for the close inspection of any individual detail in it to lead you, fairly straightforwardly, to the truth of the whole. Or, as Fredric Jameson puts it, "the possibility of realism will thus be closely related to the persistence of a certain kind of community existence, in which the experience of the individual is not yet completely sundered from the mechanisms of the socio-economic . . . Intelligibility here means that the experience of a given individual is still able to convey the structure of social life proper" ('RST', 69). But as the imperialist world-system is set into place in the later nineteenth century, such seamless space has a hole punched right through it, a gap that can never be filled. In this, the second of the "three stages of capitalist space", the realist split sets fatefully in:

> At this point the phenomenological experience of the individual subject — traditionally, the supreme raw materials of the work of art — becomes limited to a tiny corner of the social world, to a fixed camera-eye view of a certain section of London or the countryside or whatever. But the truth of that experience no longer coincides with the place in which it takes place. The truth of that limited daily experience of London lies, rather, in India or Jamaica or Hong Kong; it is bound up with the whole colonial system of the British Empire that determines the very quality of the individual's subjective life. Yet those structural coordinates are no longer accessible to immediate lived experience and are often not even conceptualizable for most people ('CM', 349).

In both *The English Novel* and *The Country and the City* Raymond Williams develops a related, though less spatially explicit, argument. At a certain moment in the late nineteenth century, in the vastly expanding metropolis and the still more immense world-system of rival imperialisms, "it was a very much longer way — impossibly longer it seemed and can still seem" from the determining international structures to immediate personal "felt life" (*EN*, 131).

Strangely enough, both *Border Country* and *Second Generation* know this well; they are realist novels which imply that realism is dead. For the theme of Empire, which has sometimes been seen as an absence in Williams's early writings, is importantly present in both novels. Matthew Price jumps on to a bus and almost into its West Indian conductress; the consequences of Empire are there from the second sentence of *Border Country*, testifying to the penetrating and warping of local space by colonialist space. As we have seen and Jameson's model predicts, Welsh space in this novel is no longer fully comprehensible from within; its lived experiences no longer coincide with the structural determinants that shape it. Its 'truth' is always elsewhere, in that very London from which, in a complacent pastoral contrast, we might be inclined to differentiate Glynmawr as knowable community; but, as Eira Rosser knows, to study Wales you have to go to London, as Matthew has. This is no less true in 1926, and realism actually lurches into a formal as well as political crisis during the General Strike, its leisurely narration breaking down into that flurry of telegrams and urgent instructions from elsewhere which make these sections of the novel as typographically distinct as they are socially tense.

Second Generation, too, is fissured by related spatial disjunctions, since for Midlands car-workers, "You damn near wonder if you exist at all, except in some bloody file in London" (*SG*, 105). Yet the book, at this national level, makes one last-ditch effort to reconstitute realist space, a knowable community. In *Politics and Letters*, Williams's interviewers complain that "the real centres of industrial power remain entirely abstract in the novel . . . The two lecturers, Lane and Dean, thus tend to function unduly as structural substitutes for a depiction of the employers" (*PL*, 289). This is surely true. Williams's novel knows that the power that determines the fate of Oxford car workers is located not in Oxford but in that distant London file; but if it admitted this to itself, it would have to abandon realism, to accept that a "knowable community" in which even the class enemy can be met in personal, face-to-face encounters no longer exists. Into this structural gap the book inserts Dean and Lane, class enemies you can sup sherry and even go to bed with if you will; it restores the coherent space of realism at the cost of considerably overestimating the function of the academy in the exercise of class power. But this somewhat desperate solution to realism's problems is once more unravelled at the international dimension. The issue of imperialism is raised repeatedly in the book, by Kate and Arthur, by Harold Owen, by Peter — a thematic preoccupation which culminates in Peter's meeting with the African nationalists at a party. To understand the experience of British industrial workers in the 1960s, the novel implies, you would somehow have to take on board the global economic structures from which these Africans have suffered; but this is an insight which, if followed through, would lead *Second Generation* beyond its realist brief altogether.

The spatial and formal problem is summed up in *The Fight for Manod*, when Matthew Price looks down over the Afren valley where an extraordinary new city may be built: "there was no route in the senses from the thousands of details, the working papers of the city, to this green valley where they might eventually be

75

realized, these fields in which thousands would build and move"
(*FM*, 37). No route in the senses: in this disjunction between
locality and social power, experience and structure, the 'truth' of a
society can no longer be given in the old realist mode, through the
patient detailing of concrete, face-to-face individual relationships.
If this was already true in the age of rival imperial nation-states and
their wars, it is even more so in the third of the three stages of
capitalist space, "our own moment, the moment of the
multinational network, or what Mandel calls 'late capitalism', a
moment in which not merely the older city but even the nation-
state itself has ceased to play a central functional and formal role"
('CM', 350). For it is just such a multi- or 'paranational' space that
The Fight for Manod and *The Volunteers* inhabit, the space of
capitalism's new drift, new indifference, as Robert Lane put it.
Manod and *The Volunteers* determinedly set out to map the
complexities of paranational space, and they therefore know right
from the start, unlike Williams's first two novels, that they *cannot*
be realist novels — though *Manod*, with its links to the earlier
works, is still partly tugged in a realist direction. In these two
'middle period' novels, there is a perfect match between Williams's
inherent spatial poetics — already finely embodied in the first two
novels despite their realist allegiance to narrating rather than
describing — and the nature of his subject-matter. For Edward
Soja has argued that in the epoch of multinational capital power
operates more through space than time, that "space makes a critical
difference, that revealing how spatial restructuring hides
consequences from us is the key to making political and theoretical
sense of the changing political economy of the contemporary" (*PG*,
62). Such restructuring, which Soja and many others have termed
'post-fordist', is indeed his second 'path of spatialisation' of
modern critical theory; and Raymond Williams in these two novels
is, we might say, its 'poet', though naturally an intensely critical
one. Spatial 'description', then, rather than realist 'narration' is by
now very much the name of the game.

★ ★ ★

The Fight for Manod is a novel written under the sign of
apocalypse, of the *dies irae* or last days. The knell of an entire

society tolls sombrely in its closing pages. This may seem surprising when we think of the mid-Wales valley the book so vividly evokes. Yet Robert Lane speaks of "a culture, a social system, an economic order, that have in fact reached their end . . . this imperial, exporting, divided order is ending" (*FM*, 181). As Matthew Price stares out of Lane's London office he seems to witness the very image of God's wrath, a token of plagues and cataclysms to come: "on the skyline of buildings there was a column of black smoke, thickening and spreading as he watched" (182). This is the very reverse of, say, D.H. Lawrence's *The Rainbow*, a symbol which announces God's covenant with his people and, in a bleak present, the promise of new life to come; Williams's column of smoke is, rather, an anti-rainbow, touching Matthew with its own doom and marking him down for that second heart attack which nearly kills him at the close of this novel.

And when we turn to the Welsh valley which is under discussion in that London office, as Price and Lane debate the plans for the new city, Manod, to be built around the actually existing village Manod in the Afren valley, we find that apocalypse has already taken place. It is as if, within the careful sociological detailing of Welsh rural depopulation, some uncanny shift of generic gears takes place in *The Fight for Manod*, so that we are in a world that is both realistic and science-fictional at once; for the most suggestive generic parallel here seems to be recent fictions of nuclear apocalypse. The Afren valley is touched at its very core by death, as Peter Owen finds when he peruses a local paper: "Births, Marriages, Deaths, in a large Gothic title. Yet they were all, incredibly, deaths" (108). The villagers call a local road junction the Wall of Death, but then, as we come grimly to realise, death is not just the name of a specific site of danger but a general condition in this valley, as if some disastrous radiation-sickness or Biblical plague (a metaphor that Williams will make literal in *People of the Black Mountains*) were sweeping through it. Old Mrs Lewis, the Prices' neighbour in their rented cottage, actually dies in the course of the novel; down the road lives Mrs Celyn, nearly ninety and confined to the house, a body so immobile that nobody really knows whether it's alive or not any more. The sickness, whatever it is, afflicts the younger generations too, in the ghastly red blotches that so disfigure the face of Gwen Vaughan or the anorexic phobias which have Juliet Dance so powerfully in their grip. There are no children — the only baby born in the course of the novel being Peter and Beth's and thus from 'outside'. As Gwen Vaughan rides past the church, "the silence now seemed to drive in on her. It was hanging in the air as if it were the only truth of the place" (51), and she has a desolating vision of the children who once inhabited the lane. "The history of this place", Matthew Price tells us, trying to steer the novel back from post-nuclear science-fiction to straight social history, "is that the young go away" (27). But against this we need to set our own sense as readers that the spaces of death are unusually prominent and active in *Manod*. The graveyard is given unwonted prominence in Williams's description of the village church; it encroaches irresistibly into Mrs Lewis's cottage, and seems even to have gained a toe-hold in the Prices', in that settled intense cold they find so difficult to drive out. The contemporary graveyard is complemented by that ancient "burial mound, grass covered, rising out of the bracken" high up on Waunfawr (54), which is no sooner described than, jealous of young life, it seems to reach out and touch Ivor Vaughan with its own deathliness, sending his tractor crashing down on top of him.

As in all fictions of nuclear apocalypse, the major social institutions and technologies are breaking rapidly down. The village school has closed, its chapel has become a barn, a final closure notice is posted on the church during the course of the book; the valley railway has closed down, there are no longer buses out to Manod, the Prices have no telephone in their cottage. In Nantlais, further down the valley, "there had been no development outwards, and little building of any kind, in the last sixty years" (29). High up on the mountains, "there were a score of ruins, within a morning's walk: the nettles growing thickly inside the crumbling walls" (161). Elsewhere in the Wales of this novel, Glynmawr station has been bulldozed down into hardcore and Morgan Rosser's jam factory has declined into a tyre depot; "none of it felt like change; it felt like cancellation" (29). Even language seems to be seizing up or slowing down, as if regressing to some more rudimentary level of monosyllabic grunts and gestures. "Able", remarks Bryn Walters thoughtfully, "that's a word I haven't heard used in a long time" (30), and Gethin Jenkins seems often to have left the realms of articulacy for good.

The lost world of Manod — "on a plateau, almost hidden from below . . . still in many ways remote" (21) — may even belong, in another generic shift, to the realms of horror fiction and the Gothic novel. It is akin to those sinister villages upon which a belated traveller stumbles and has no choice but to stay, villages populated as one faintly suspects from the beginning but only terrifyingly confirms later by the undead, who seek to draw the reluctant guest into their own world of voodoo and abomination. Our first glimpse of Manod is through Matthew's eyes just before dawn, in a mode of writing peculiar to this novel which leaves realism far behind and verges on something between sublimity and barely suppressed terror.

> But now there were only these growing outlines of shadow, in a world as yet without detail, without colour. He felt a certain awe, a certain coldness, as he continued to watch. What he saw in this country, which he believed he knew, was very deeply unfamiliar, a waiting strangeness, as if it was not yet known what world would come out of these shadows, what new world, that begins every day (20).

Later, as Matthew and Susan drive in the mountains, they seem to experience what Gaston Bachelard terms "an ear that knows how to dream" (*PS*, 166): "they felt the air pressure change, in their ears; it sounded like the coming of another dimension of hearing" (174). In the clashing linguistic registers of this one sentence, the discrepant genres which inhabit this novel battle it out to a tense stand-off: realism's scientific explanations (air pressure) wrestle with the language of apocalypse (the coming of another dimension). On Pontafren bridge Matthew stumblingly seeks to explain to Peter Owen metamorphoses which are both physical and generic: "You feel it here, do you? . . . Something different. Something other. Some altered physical sense . . . Something that actually alters me" (97). The most vivid 'alteration' in the novel is in those extraordinary and obscure pages in which, alone in the valley, Matthew suddenly becomes the most formidable bearer of death in the entire novel, suffering "a long mourning through all the reaches of his body". We here leave behind the realm of realism and detail for an uncanny zone of elementality and myth in which, in a sense stronger than conventional metaphors of tradition and continuity, he physically becomes his father: "a heavy possession, self-possession beyond the ordinary self: the immediate detail just barely dealt with, as if hearing and seeing only sound and light" (37).

In this eerie zone of sickness, technological involution and death, this 'other dimension' of transfigured bodies and alarming archetypes, strange creatures live, act, and have their being: Gethin Jenkins, who in his dour taciturnity, his financial graspingness, his constant aura of menace and occasional acts of gratuitous sadism, seems to have walked straight into this novel from the pages of *Wuthering Heights*; Judith Dance, locked in an inner world of tormenting obsessions, starving herself slowly to death in the vicarage; even the normally genial Modlen, metamorphosed into a bedraggled, nocturnal 'madwoman' ("Aye, and I'll do something wild", 95) by Gethin's treatment of her. But the Queen of the Goths, surely, is Gwen Vaughan, a figure of intense psychic and physical violence whose first appearance in the novel is her "extraordinary gallop" on Cavalier down the village lane. Alienated from adult heterosexuality ("she couldn't bear him touching her", 50), incestuously fixated on her dead father who, like Harry Price, seems constantly on the point of rematerialising ("she looked again at the empty chair by the fire", 49), acting as a savagely possessive and perhaps sexually jealous mother to her much younger brother Ivor, vaguely lesbian in her 'butch' close-cropped hair, abandonment of conventionally feminine dress and passion for hard, 'male' riding, the spectacularly disfigured Gwen is one of the most extraordinary creations in all of Williams's fiction. Kate Owen, in the realist novel *Second Generation*, disturbed us because of her adultery, in a wholly human pattern of relationships; Gwen Vaughan, in the generically indeterminate *Manod*, disturbs because she is, in my view, a witch.

Gwen materialises from the magician's traditional cloud of smoke, as when, quite unexpectedly, "Susan, staring past the smoke, saw Gwen Vaughan standing there" (197). But the rational explanation, as ever, does not quite quell the sense of another dimension of meaning here. More sinister is her visit to the farming family whose daughter Ivor hopes to marry, which at once marks down for death the young lives that inhabit the farm. Mrs Parry's basket of tabby kittens will "have to be got rid of, but not just yet"; but Gwen, in her obsessive attention to them — "standing over the kittens . . . stared down at the kittens" (52) — sinisterly seems to bring this lethal moment perceptibly closer. The nearest literary analogue here is Maggie Tulliver in George Eliot's *The Mill on the Floss*, another paternal favourite whose ability unwittingly to deal death to her pets has been seen as evidence, in feminist re-readings of this novel, as part of a network of witch or vampire imagery that attaches to her. Gwen's most impressive piece of witchery, however, concerns humans, not animals. I noted above that the ancient burial mound encroaches upon living space and sends Ivor's tractor toppling down on him, but what I omitted from that account is the fact that it is Gwen, picking her way through the ancient grave on Cavalier, who seems to function as the very catalyst of the accident, as if her physical presence in the grave completed some deadly 'electrical' circuit between it and her brother's body. Forcing Ivor back into a dependency on his sister he was threatening to grow out of, the accident accords well enough with Gwen's unconscious wishes, and its nature — the trapping and breaking of Ivor's leg — links it with the castration symbolism familiar from women's Gothic fiction, of which the blinding of Rochester in *Jane Eyre* is the most famous instance. Around this bizarre array of Gothic characters a Gothic architecture struggles to shape itself, in the novel's references to "old rotting dark passages" (40), the "old curving staircase" (60), or that derelict kitchen of Gethin's farm which again might have come straight out of *Wuthering Heights*.

Into this waste land of goths and ghouls, ruins and redundancy, comes an ageing Matthew Price, as official consultant for the newly revived government scheme to build the new city in the Afren valley. I shall say more about the city below, but want first to discuss its subjective rather than objective meaning, to consider it as a fantasy of habitation on Matthew's part akin to Kate Owen's nest. A remark of Gaston Bachelard's can give us a start here:

> Sometimes the house of the future is better built, lighter and larger than all the houses of the past, so that the image of *the dream house* is opposed to that of the childhood home. Late in life, with indomitable courage, we continue to say that we are going to do what we have not yet done: we are going to build a house . . . Maybe it is a good thing for us to keep a few dreams of a house that we shall live in later, always later, so much later, in fact, that we shall not have time to achieve it (*PS*, 61).

'Late in life': this is our first connection with Matthew Price, whose children have grown up and who has suffered his first heart attack before the opening of *The Fight for Manod*. The 'dream house' is our second link, for we later find Matthew and Susan excitedly kneeling on the floor in front of a set of cottage conversion plans, "imagining and discussing the fine house that could in this way be built around them" (167). "What a dynamic, handsome object is a path!" exclaims Bachelard (*PS*, 11), and Matthew Price agrees, since one of the first things we learn about him in his Manod cottage is that "he carried out the ash and spread it, carefully, on the path he was making down the back garden" (24). Paths become important in *Manod* as a smallscale version of that spatial 'mapping out' which was crucial in *Border Country* and emerges forcefully again as a theme here. The tensions-to-come in Matthew's relations with the local builder John Dance are signalled early on when the latter unwittingly occupies the ash path, ousting Matthew from his self-made territory; and Susan and her sons recognise its significance after Matthew's second heart attack:

"He laid this path, did he?" Jack asked.
"Yes, from the fires".
"As if he was staying here" (197).

The ash path is the only actual 'building' Matthew does in the novel; yet the theme of building, we come to realise, preoccupies the book. "There's not enough training, anywhere, in building", Matthew laments to Dance (39); and even later when he has vastly more important things on his mind he always knocks off for the odd chat with builders; "as they walked through to the house he spoke to the men on the scaffolding" (175). And the prominence in the book of John Dance — who is indeed, as Matthew dryly notes, "into everything" as both local builder and agent for the multinational companies that are moving stealthily into the Afren valley (75) — further testifies to the imaginative grip of builders and buildings on Williams's novel.

In the long run, indeed, *The Fight for Manod* turns into a battle between two ageing builders, the purely mental builder Matthew Price and the actual builder John Dance. Certainly one of its finest scenes is that in which Matthew finally confronts Dance head-on in the vicarage, returning the latter's conversion plans and throwing back in his face the bribe they implicitly represented. And as the ageing builder confronts his adversary we realise how deeply Williams's novel is in the grip of a text by a playwright to whom his relationship was in his early years, by his own account, obsessive: Henrik Ibsen's *The Master Builder* (1892). It was, perhaps, no accident that Peter Owen was in Scandinavia at the start of *Manod*.

Matthew Price, in effect, is Halvard Solness, Master Builder, girding himself to one last stupendous architectural effort before old age and then death dim the radiance of his constructive powers. John Dance is then a composite figure in terms of the play, combining both Knut Brovnik, the ageing builder ousted by Solness (for the Manod project would sweep away Dance's self-interested hopes for the development of a modest new estate), and his son Ragnar who actively challenges Solness (since Matthew is ailing, Dance vigorous). Other motifs also carry over from play to novel: Ibsen's spires are echoed by Williams's towers, and the odd, inconsequential fascination of scaffolding in both *Second Generation* and *Manod* may echo its importance in Ibsen (Solness falls to his death from it). What is absent from the novel is the element of sexual attraction between the ageing Master Builder and his female devotees, Kaja Fosli and then Hilde Wangel. Only an odd early scene where Matthew gives Modlen a lift into town, and a crude Freudian symbolism (her bag, his keys) comes fleetingly into play, even glances in this direction, though as we shall see the relation between Mark Evans and his much younger wife in *The Volunteers* develops this motif in full.

Williams's Master Builder, however, has rather grander plans than Ibsen's. Where Solness, in his last great feat of building, merely adds an enormous spire to a dwelling house, Matthew Price aspires to found an entire new city before darkness and death close round him. This, indeed, is the profoundest fantasy of habitation at work in *The Fight for Manod*, a rewriting of Peter Owen's shell or his mother's nest on a gigantic scale. "No one but you should be allowed to build. Only you", cries Hilde Wangel to Ibsen's Solness (*P*, 281); but in *Manod* Tom Weinberg criticises rather than shares in what he sees as spatial megalomania on Matthew Price's part, "these oversize ambitions that are wearing you down . . . To be arbiter, now, of that valley and that city" (188). This arbitership is actually achieved in the spatial structure of the novel. Its first half has Matthew driving restlessly through the valley to interview people, its second part shows him presiding in his cottage while others increasingly bring their problems to him. Nor need he be mistaken in thinking he can found a city. A former research student writes to convey "the sense so many of us have that you founded us" (131), and through his teaching and example Matthew effectively has founded that new Institute and Library of Industrial Wales whose directorship he eventually accepts. And always he dreams of it — a city we shall live in later, always later, so much later that he will never have time to achieve it:

> He could close his eyes and then open them on the city in the valley. The grey cluster of works at St Dyfrog. At Llanerch and Manod, at Bronydd and Fforest and Parc-y-Meirch and the Cwm, terraces of houses, central white towers. Circles of white light at the road intersections. The traffic, the sound, of a hundred thousand people (37).

This is a vision to beggar the imagination of Master Builder Solness; and in a novel in which the "other dimension" is so palpably present, in which you really do not know "what world would come out of these shadows, what new world", why should it *not* come suddenly into being, just as the nest Kate's body longed for took on actual shape and form through Arthur Dean's uncle?

What kind of city would it be if it did? An unlikely convergence between Matthew Price and Gaston Bachelard again points to an answer. The former likes sitting in semi-darkness, since he "grew up in a house without electric light. That hard glare, overhead, always presses in on me" (77). The latter doesn't have much use for modern lighting either, afraid "lest our indirect lighting cause us to lose the center of the room" which the evening lamp on the family table used to be (*PS*, 171). Modern lighting is just one instance for Bachelard of a wholesale loss of human, intimate space in the spatially rationalised contemporary city, and a key issue for him is: "how can one help confer greater cosmicity upon the city space . . . ?" (*PS*, 28). His answer, a technique of meditation for transforming Paris into a 'city-ocean', is a fanciful, idealist one; but the issue he raises, of urban space and 'cosmicity', is central to *Manod*, as it was becoming in the culture at large in the years that Williams worked on the novel.

As Master Builder Price patiently digs out old plants in his garden, his arch-rival Dance announces: "Get a bulldozer in, that's what we usually do. Clear the old muck right out, all the old roots and drains" (*FM*, 122). We can let the remark resonate beyond its local context and remind us of the project of modernist architecture and the Enlightenment reason that underpins it. Abolish local customs, reject antiquated 'prejudices', clear from your mind and bulldoze down in reality the historical styles of other epochs, start absolutely anew, follow only the 'reason' or logic of materials and function, letting nothing subjective sway you from this uncompromising, austere path. The result of this programme would be a Le Corbusier mansion or Mies van der Rohe skyscraper, though after the mass-destruction of World War Two it became possible to reconstruct whole districts or even cities according to functionalist principles. In *The Condition of Post-modernity* David Harvey notes that "it was almost as if a new and revivified version of the Enlightenment project sprang, phoenix-like, out of the death and destruction of global conflict", and the keynote of this urban reconstruction was *reason*, the "rationalization of spatial patterns and circulating systems" (*CP*, 68–69). Such rigorous planning would be carried out by an avant-garde of architects which sees itself as threatened on three fronts: by physical nature, in its rich diversity and sprawling 'illogic'; by the disparate clutter (as they see it) of what the city historically contains, the "old muck" which can't always be obliterated as conveniently as Glynmawr station; and finally by the 'masses', those illiterate consumers of architecture who actually dare to like traditional local styles or the commercial, mass-cultural fashions of the present. This kind of spatial planning is thus exemplary of the social relations of modernist art in general, in which an avant-garde elite always glared defiantly out at the despised masses beyond it — an elite which includes T.S. Eliot and Ezra Pound as well as Le Corbusier and Mies van der Rohe.

Architectural modernism scorns the irrationalities of Nature, tradition and popular taste; and it is then not surprising that *post*modernism, which first emerges in the field of architecture, should aim to vindicate these excluded terms. Typical manifestos include Robert Venturi's *Learning from Las Vegas* (1972), which insists that architects creatively engage the city of commerce, kitsch and mass-cultural cliché rather than loftily turning their backs on it, and Tom Wolfe's *From Bauhaus to Our House* (1981), which rejects the spartan functionalism of Walter Gropius in favour of local vernacular building traditions, of a place-specific rather than universalist architecture, such as the 'prairie architecture' of Frank Lloyd Wright based on the terrain of the American mid-West. Postmodernism is thus an aesthetic *populism*, reaffirming historical and mass-cultural or 'user-friendly' styles while at the same time not simply abandoning some of the tough, critical questions that modernism posed to these. It is, specifically, post- and not anti-modernism, not a simple revivalism. And long before *The Fight for Manod* Raymond Williams's work participated in this postmodern populist shift. Combating modernist elitism in *Culture and Society*, he famously declared that "we live in an expanding culture, yet we spend much of our energy regretting the fact, rather than seeking to understand its nature and conditions" (*CS*, viii), and much of his early writing challenges the dismissive modernist notion of 'the masses'. Williams's well-known slogan of 1958, "Culture is Ordinary", deserves setting alongside Robert Venturi and Tom Wolfe's catchy titles as a defence of popular creativity against avant-garde contempt for it; and the very discipline of 'cultural studies', which emerged from Williams's work and broke down modernism's high art/mass culture distinction, can be seen as a typical postmodernist phenomenon.

Culture and Society can even be seen, in some senses, as a sketch for *The Fight for Manod* itself. For its discussion of Edmund Burke, which uses him against the 'top-down', dominative nature of Enlightenment planning and yet is unwilling simply to endorse his own conservatism, precisely parallels the extended, difficult meditation on planning in *Manod* itself. How can we move beyond modernist elitism, to a more participatory, popular, historically aware mode of planning without simply losing sight of the moment of truth in modernism, its necessary testing of local traditions against the yardstick of universal reason? Williams's formulations in *The English Novel* and elsewhere of a necessary dialectic, a permanent if painful interaction of 'traditional community' and 'educated consciousness', is a recasting of just this issue; and the 'border country' between these two poles, where both must be impossibly sustained, is remarkably close to some definitions of postmodern architecture. In his influential *The Language of Post-Modern Architecture*, for instance, Charles Jencks uses the terms 'schizophrenia' or 'double coding' to convey the force of Williams's border country. A postmodern building, Jencks argues, "is, if a short definition is needed, one which speaks on at least two levels at once: to other architects, to a concerned minority [and] to the public at large, or the local inhabitants . . . The buildings most characteristic of post-modernism show a marked duality, a conscious schizophrenia" (*LPA*, 6). As we shall see, the new city in Williams's novel is 'double-coded' in just this way.

Postmodernism, then, is populist and historicist, querying modernism's ruthless desire to start absolutely anew and finding inspiration in Nature, local traditions and popular tastes. But it is also, as many theorists have agreed, importantly to do with *space*. Fredric Jameson declares that "a certain spatial turn offers one of the more productive ways of distinguishing postmodernism from modernism proper" ('UPU', 11). This "spatial turn" has on occasion been seen in negative terms. Yes, postmodernism returns to the architectural styles of the past, but it does so only in a spirit of witty, self-regarding pastiche, reducing history to a play of glossy, eclectic surfaces, to a depthless space akin to the 'image' in *Border Country*. This danger is real enough, but more recently post-modernism's spatial orientation has come to be guardedly welcomed. Jameson, who was sharply critical of postmodern 'depthlessness' in his early essays on the subject, now accepts that "spatialization . . . whatever it may take away in the capacity to think time and History, also opens a door on to a whole new domain for libidinal investment of the Utopian and even protopolitical type" ('UPU', 17). And postmodernism is the third of Edward Soja's three paths of spatialisation in *Postmodern Geographies*, after the reassessment of space in social theory (post-historicism) and its renewed importance in contemporary capitalist restructuring (post-fordism). This last of his spatialisations is, he argues, "couched in a cultural and ideological reconfiguration, a changing definition of the experiential meaning of modernity, the emergence of a new, postmodern culture of space and time" (*PG*, 62). And this new visibility of space in postmodernist culture has played a key role in the reformulation of Marxist theory by geographers such as

87

Soja and David Harvey, leading directly to their demands for a "topian Marxism" or a "historico-geographical materialism".

By orientating my discussions of *Border Country* and *Second Generation* around space and the socio-spatial dialectic, I was thus already treating Raymond Williams as some sort of postmodern novelist, as a remarkable precursor of concerns we have come to see as distinctively postmodernist. But in *The Country and the City* (1973) and *The Fight for Manod* he addresses these concerns much more directly. *The Country and the City* has often been seen as a decisive 'break' in his oeuvre, as informed by a harsher political anger than the early writing and as a major rapprochement between Williams and Marxism. But if Williams moved towards Marxism, so did Marxism move towards him, in its new interests in the city and the "specificity of the urban". Edward Soja writes of "the coalition of geographers, sociologists and political economists that had formed in the 1970s to develop a new critical interpretation of capitalist urbanization" (*PG*, 69). Key works of this coalition would include Henri Lefebvre's *La Révolution Urbaine* (1970) and *La Pensée Marxiste et la Ville* (1972), Manuel Castell's *La Question Urbaine* (1972) and David Harvey's *Social Justice and the City* (1974). And from this initial focus on the specific nature of city space emerges that general concern with the socially formative nature of space which is characteristic of 'postmodern Marxism'. In *La Révolution Urbaine* Henri Lefebvre claims that "space and the political organization of space express social relationships but also react back upon them . . . Industrialization, once the producer of urbanism, is now being produced by it" (cited in *PG*, 76), and two years later, in 1974, he published his masterwork, *The Production of Space*.

As Raymond Williams and Marxism were converging around the theme of the city in the mid-seventies, postmodernism was heading in the same direction. For once you have rejected the arrogant dualisms of modernism — avantgarde building versus the degraded city fabric around it — the very notion of a 'building' expands and opens out. The postmodern building must be *integrated* into its urban context, must respond with equal measures of wit, sensitivity and enthusiasm to the various historical or mass-cultural styles surrounding it. Like the space of 'home' in *Border Country*, the concept of 'building' in postmodernism cannot be confined to the single artefact; it is an intensely relational or contextual one, expanding far out into urban space in general, and thus pointing the social thinking of postmodernism inevitably towards the theme of the city. In 1972 Robert Venturi's *Learning from Las Vegas* already offered a new model city — not the rationalised, functionalist spaces of the modernist city underpinned, in Charles Jencks's pungent phrase, by a "clean, salubrious hospital metaphor" (*LPA*, 9), but a city of vibrant mass-cultural energy and witty commercial cliché. In the same year Rem Koolhaas and Zoe Zenghelis painted *The City of the Captive Globe*, a wonderful vision of New York as mass-cultural, multi-ethnic metropolis, diverse, fragmented and above all vibrant, containing within itself the bustling styles and cultures of the entire globe. In 1974 Jonathan Raban proposed the notion of 'soft city' in a book of that title, arguing that the 'hard city' of modernist rational planning had had its day and that urban space was now a rich, crowded field for the production of signs, images, fantasy, a space of aesthetics and stylising; we shall see later how relevant such ideas are to *The Volunteers*. In 1975 Colin Rowe formulated the important concept of 'Collage City', a space of chance, collision and the 'irrational' in contrast to the relentlessly logical modernist city. He found a smallscale model for his concept in Hadrian's Villa, of which he writes:

> the Villa Adriana attempts to dissimulate all reference to a single controlling idea . . . Hadrian, who proposes the reverse of any 'totality', seems only to need the accumulation of the most various fragments . . . The Villa Adriana is a miniature Rome. It plausibly reproduces all the collisions of set pieces and all the random empirical happenings which the city so lavishly exhibited . . . It is almost certain that the uninhibited aesthetic preference of today is for the structural discontinuities and the multiple syncopated excitements which the Villa Adriana enacts (cited in *LPA*, 111).

Decentred, dispersed and haphazard, Collage City is everything that Le Corbusier, Walter Gropius and Mies van der Rohe despise; and that the aesthetic preference of today was indeed for such multiple urban discontinuities seemed confirmed by a sudden cluster of postmodern novels featuring such cities: Donald Barthelme's *City Life* (1970), Italo Calvino's *Invisible Cities* (1972),

89

the Berlin of Thomas Pynchon's *Gravity's Rainbow* (1973), William Burrough's *Cities of the Red Night* (1981) and also, perhaps, that distinctly 'invisible' because as yet unbuilt city, Raymond Williams's *Manod*.

In *The Country and the City* Williams had already found resources in both the Marxist and utopian socialist traditions for a decisive intellectual break with the modernist city. In Engels's account of socialism as "abolishing the contrast between town and country, which has been brought to its extreme point by present-day capitalist society", Williams discovers "a formulation which is at once the most exciting, the most relevant and yet the most undeveloped in the whole revolutionary argument" — though, as he notes, the utopian socialists had been here before Engels, and Williams Morris "continued to think in this way" (*CC*, 365). But the reference to Morris, whom Williams elsewhere criticises for over-simplifying the utopian society he sketches, alerts us to a problem. If the oppositions of city and country or avantgarde building and contemptible urban context are to be overcome, what guarantees that their unravelling will be fully postmodernist, and not just a pre- or anti-modernist happy Hobbitland? *The Country and the City* does not offer an answer, but *The Fight for Manod*, taking the argument one stage further, I think does.

The novel registers a powerful nostalgic drive on Matthew Price's part towards an unaltered landscape, "the warmth, the heaviness, of a known past: a green past, in which lives have been lived and completed" (*FM*, 38). Yet it and he know that this past cannot be recovered; indeed, the novel's own generic trans-formations — Gothic or horror fiction, post-nuclear apocalypse — are a sombre warning of what awaits this devastated valley if its future is after all blocked. The city that is being planned for it is, clearly, a postmodernist, decentred one, an unprecedented kind of space in which old demarcations such as 'urban' and 'rural' are fading away into irrelevance:

> Manod's in the middle, that's how it gave its name. And because the Afren floods, and because in any case we don't want a ribbon along the banks of the river, the centres are set back on the higher ground: hill-towns really, except St Dyfrog, which has a different role. Each of the cities would go up to ten thousand. Between each, as you see, at least four or five miles of quite open country,

which would go on being farmed. So what you get, as a whole, is a city of a hundred, a hundred-and-twenty thousand people, but a city of small towns, a city of villages almost. A city settling into its country (13).

Manod would thus be a city which restores that lost cosmicity or integration with elemental natural forces which Gaston Bachelard desired. The key postmodernist motifs of discontinuity and fragmentation also feature prominently in the project: it is "a working model of a different kind of city: a dispersed city" (77), just as it will both manufacture and exemplify in practice "dispersed production control processes" (191); it is, we might say, a post-fordist city. Manod is "what they call the cluster city" (157), a set of discontinuous settlements which, like Colin Rowe's Collage City, are "the reverse of any 'totality' ". And that it is also Jonathan Raban's 'soft city', a space of desire and fantasy rather than hard logic, is already clear from the intensity of Matthew Price's fantasy of being its Master Builder.

Manod is 'soft', I suspect, in a further sense too. One of the most remarkable suggestions of Bachelard's *The Poetics of Space* is that, at some deep level of fantasy, every dreamer of space envisions a utopian "space-substance" which evokes the very feel and texture of the spaces of topophilia. He cites the cases of Joë Bousquet, who "has shown us a space-substance, honey-space or space-honey", and of Philippe Diolé, whose space-substance is brine: "I moved about in the heart of a fluid, luminous, beneficent, dense matter, which was sea-water, or rather the memory of sea-water" (*PS*, 202, 207). Matthew Price doesn't quite go for a wallow in a giant vat of honey, although since the utopian space-substance is so often imaged by a thick, viscous liquid, we might want to ask ourselves again just why in *Border Country* his father's bees and hives are so important for him. In *Manod*, we find a related set of images. As Matthew talks to Peter Owen, who inhabits an Enlightenment space of pure speed and non-friction (the first time he appears in the book he's hurtling through Sweden at eighty miles per hour), he pushes "with his stick at the film of glazed mud on the edge of the lane. It was a beautiful soft pink where it had begun to dry" (*FM*, 74). Neither wholly wet nor wholly dry, the mud occupies some indeterminate state of being, some 'border country' of substances which in its sluggish viscosity deeply appeals to this novel. *Manod* is full of substances entering this sticky, clotted liminal state: of liquids thickened to the point of passing over into solids ("a rush of drain-grey liquid, with the curd and scum of used soap and scraps of food", 39; the river Afren "a milky light brown with all the soil it was carrying", 145); or, in the other direction, of solids moistening to the point where they almost become heavy liquids ("Susan felt the fibres of the wood, at first rough like worn skin but then yielding and pulpy, like hands kept too long in water", 100). This may then explain why the old water butt was such a compelling image in *Border Country* and recurs as a memory in *Manod*, since with its "soaked wood and stagnant water" (205), it neatly combines the liquefying solid and the solidifying liquid in one.

'Soft' in several senses then, the new city, Manod, is certainly non-modernist. But is it also *post*modernist, integrating rather than just cancelling modernism out? The answer, surely, is yes. For Manod is both more *and* less natural than .its modernist counterpart: it will settle into its country, but also be equipped with gadgets and technology that make Robert Lane's cluttered kitchen look stone-age in comparison. There isn't anywhere, Lane enthuses, "a city like this . . . conceived, from the beginning, in post-industrial terms and with a post-electronic technology" (13), those "new communications and transport technologies" which will precisely enable it to be a postmodernist "dispersed city" (77). In modernism, technology erases the human in the name of a stringent impersonality; in postmodernism, however, it restores it, allowing Manod to be simultaneously both smallscale ecological commune and glittering technopolis. And the novel then turns into a political meditation on the postmodern city itself, dramatising alternative possible responses through Peter Owen and Matthew Price. Peter, rather like Marxist critics in the early stages of postmodernism, tends to see the new city as nothing but an ideological blind, as capitalism's latest and most devious ruse. Matthew is alert to this possibility, but — like those postmodern Marxist geographers Edward Soja and David Harvey or a later, spatially 'repentant' Fredric Jameson — sees a utopian promise in the new kind of city, a possible break beyond the dead-ends and one-sidedness of modernist culture. *The Fight for Manod*, as it subtly plays these two contrasting responses off against each other, is not just *about* a postmodernist city; it rather in its own form *enacts* the dilemmas of the cultural critic of postmodernism. The unwieldy interpretive framework I have invoked to read it — Soja, Harvey, Jameson, Venturi — is in this sense contained within the novel itself, which, in a rare but highly effective fictional move, actually offers us the cultural critic as postmodern hero.

* * *

In *The Long Revolution* Williams wrote of what he terms the 'social-formula' novel which, unlike the more traditional 'social documentary', abstracts a pattern or formula from contemporary society and then creates its own society from that pattern. The simplest examples, he notes, "are in the field of the future-story, where the 'future' device (usually only a device, for nearly always it is contemporary society that is being written about; indeed this is becoming the main way of writing about social experience) removes the ordinary tension between the selected pattern and normal observation"; the mode also includes, importantly, "nearly all serious 'science fiction' " (*LR*, 307). From the censorious discussion of the form here, one would have been hard pressed to predict that seventeen years later Williams would himself be writing a "future-story", *The Volunteers*, published in 1978 but set ten years ahead of itself in 1988, during world economic recession and with an authoritarian coalition government in power in Britain. Moreover, packed with gadgetry as it is (helicopters and jets, television satellites, photocopiers and fax-machines, electronic bug detectors, community video, pay-as-you-watch television in station waiting rooms), *The Volunteers* seems constantly to be hovering on the verge of full science fiction, as if this were the genre that in its heart of hearts it truly aspired to.

At the very centre of these assorted technologies is television. The hero of *The Volunteers*, Lewis Redfern, is a consultant analyst on the political underground for Insatel, an international satellite television service. The book's central event — the terrorist shooting of cabinet Minister Buxton in the Welsh Folk Museum at St Fagans — is conceived of as 'televisual' from the very start; and one of Redfern's key antagonists, Rosa Brant, was once a programme director with the new Fifth Channel. Television had already featured importantly in *Second Generation*. There it was, by turns, an index of the new affluent society, an important new force in shaping public attitudes to industrial disputes, a source of abstract spatial pleasures in its own right ("the outline shapes continually developing and interlocking" on the screen, *SG*, 15), an unsettling technology of spatial disjunction when you "come in off the street and straight out to Montana" (14) and, finally, a deep though undefined menace to identity. Television serves very early on as a signal of Peter Owen's own inner disturbance, of a multiplying and then fracturing of identity. For only moments after he passes the vacant simulacrum of a room in the furniture store, he stares "next door, in the radio shop" where "five television sets demonstrated an identical image in unequal sizes" (11). Those dangerous photographic 'images' of *Border Country* are now, clearly, on the move.

Whereas television in *Second Generation* remains a matter of theme, as one interesting contemporary phenomenon among many others, in *The Volunteers* it is both theme and form, in ways which raise issues central to postmodernism. I have so far discussed postmodernism in terms of populism; and as a major new cultural technology, enjoying immense popularity, unsettling high-cultural traditionalists and even challenging the hegemony of the book itself, television fits neatly enough into this framework. But as a powerful technology of cultural *reproduction* it has, along with film, tape recording and video, given rise to an alternative account of the postmodern, in terms of the "society of the spectacle" (Guy Debord) or the "logic of the simulacrum" (Jean Baudrillard). In the good old days, this account runs, reproductive technology merely mirrored a real world which pre-existed it. The reflection or image might tell us additional things we didn't know about reality, but no one was likely to confuse the two, to take image for reality; the realist novel is perhaps exemplary here. But as reproductive cultural technologies multiply in our own century, the balance of power between reality and image shifts. The image emerges from its secondary role and threatens to overpower or even, paradoxically, to construct the very 'reality' of which it was supposed to be a copy; Marilyn Monroe, say, is an image vastly more culturally significant and thus 'real' than the actual suffering woman who was her pretext. We enter a baffling new world which Jean Baudrillard describes as follows:

> Abstraction today is no longer that of the map, the double, the mirror or the concept. Simulation is no longer that of a territory, a referential being or a substance. It is the generation by models of a real without origin or reality: a hyperreal. The territory no longer precedes the map, nor survives it. Henceforth it is the map that precedes the territory — *precession of simulacra* — it is the map that engenders the territory (*SW*, 166).

That which was secondary becomes primary; what was once primary is now, strangely, nothing but the copy of its own copy. But this uncanny postmodernist disturbance of the relation between the copy and the copied had already infiltrated Welsh ɔpace in *The Fight for Manod*, where a passage that begins conventionally enough ends up by metamorphosing Juliet Dance into a simulacrum:

> she seemed a rare prototype, which human figures only occasionally achieve, of the beauty of the figurine or the doll . . . the perfection so often achieved by the conscious hand, in porcelain or in paint. But there was no way of knowing whether such figures were imitations, records, of the rare Juliets who had appeared, unexpectedly, in the crowded generations, or whether the occasional Juliet . . . was not a human repetition, an imitation in its turn, of the dolls and the figurines (*FM*, 111–12).

A supposed original turns out to be no more than an imitation of its own imitation, and this alarming process of 'Julietisation', this precession of simulacra, is generalised by television across a whole society in *The Volunteers*. Insatel, a "network already installed for spectacle", actually *creates* most of the 'reality' it claims merely to mirror; "most of the events, of course, Insatel arranges itself: all the big sporting contests, the festivals, the exhibitions" (*V*, 6).

History too has become subject to the laws of postmodern 'hyper-reality' in the Welsh Folk Museum which so dominates the opening of *The Volunteers*. This open-air museum, with its reconstructed farmhouses, cockpit and customs house, its "simulated peace of a village" (15), claims to be the neutral reproduction of an actual history. In the event, however, it constructs that which it claims to copy, turning real men and women into mere "polished shells of their lives" (29). Like *Second Generation*, *The Volunteers* opens with an empty, simulated room, as Lewis Redfern sits "facing the collection of old ladles and carving knives, in a kitchen which had everything but food" to hear a police briefing in the museum castle after the terrorist attack (10). This transformation of history into tourist or spectator space by the museum, its "spatial logic of the simulacrum" (Fredric Jameson's phrase), belongs to a trend which many commentators have noted as a typically postmodern one: the emergence of 'theme parks' and 'heritage industry'. David Harvey, for instance, regards "the growth of a museum culture (in Britain a museum opens every three weeks, and in Japan 500 have opened up in the last fifteen years)" as a significant index of that "condition of postmodernity" which he aims to diagnose (*CPM*, 62).

We might then be inclined (Redfern himself is at one point) to draw a sharp contrast between the sanitised and 'spatialised' world of the Folk Museum and the shooting of Buxton that takes place inside it. But we would be wrong to do so, and terrorism too belongs to the "society of the spectacle". Already in 1972, writing of the grim events at the Munich Olympics when seventeen people were killed in a shoot-out between Palestinian hostage-takers and German security forces, Raymond Williams asked bitterly, "Is terrorism becoming a spectator sport?" (*RWT*, 21). The answer, as *The Volunteers* well knows, is: yes. Terrorism is not some pristine, brutal reality which television then happens upon and reports; it is, rather, from the very start, conceived as a reality-to-be-televised, an action that is simultaneously an image. Television has, so to speak, constitutively entered the terrorist attack; it creates the terrorist, not reflects him. Or as Baudrillard puts it, "all hold ups, hijacks and the like are now as it were simulation hold ups, in the sense that they are inscribed in advance in the decoding and orchestration rituals of the media" (*SW*, 179).

Williams's term for "hyper-reality" or "society of the spectacle" is the "dramatized society", coined in his Cambridge inaugural lecture of 1974. There he notes that with the advent of television a qualitative cultural leap sets in: drama is no longer a local or occasional production of images, but rather "in quite new ways, is built into the rhythms of everyday life . . . Till the eyes tire, millions of us watch the shadows of shadows and find them substance" (*WS*, 13). Beyond the overt "theatricality of our image-conscious public world", we have, he claims, entered a new phase of "the dramatization of consciousness itself" (17–18). The most dramatised or image-ridden of all societies, no doubt, is the United States, and as visiting professor at Stanford University in 1972, Raymond Williams found himself ensconced in the postmodern heartlands; it was here, in a truly addictive television culture, that he began work on *Television: Technology and Cultural Form*, whose central concept of 'total flow' has been repeatedly invoked by later theorists of postmodernity. But there is nothing specifically American about the 'dramatised society' in *The Volunteers*, whose young terrorists are well versed in image, simulacrum and spectacle. Lewis Redfern soon realises that the shooting of Buxton in the legs has been "drama as a moment of significant public action", that the police reconstruction "was of an initially staged event", and he resolves to head back to London to do "a little updated study of the radical theatre" (*V*, 59–60). Later, in yet another of a long series of empty simulacra, the terrorists set in place "a stage-set, in effect, of a young revolutionary's 'hide-out' " for the police to discover (62). If any of this novel's non-rooms were actually occupied, they would no doubt contain the body that graces its paperback edition: that fair-haired, bearded young man in an orange mountain cape and armed with a shot-gun, a body which is in fact even more vacantly simulacral than Juliet Dance's own. Strip the disguise away and what we find, in effect, is television: Rosa Brant, veteran of closed circuit student television and ex-Channel Five director; Rosa who, in the military storming of the Pontyrhiw power depot four months earlier, had already told the television crew that they were filming from the wrong (i.e. police) side of the barricades.

If, as Jean Baudrillard claims, in postmodernism the map precedes the territory it models, then the task of cartography becomes even more important in Williams's fiction. In *The Fight for Manod* Matthew Price was confronted early on with a map of the project — that "map on the high glass screen" in Lane's office (*FM*, 12), which he must then turn back into a human itinerary in the Afren valley, and Lewis Redfern readily inserts himself into the great tradition of Williamsite cartographers: "I'm what they call a consultant analyst. That means making maps: political maps" (*V*, 24). However, if we edge the image of the map in a spatial rather than social direction (or, better, in a socio-spatial one) and try some

97

mapping out of our own, we shall see that the entire novel is constructed around two spatial axes: the verticality of domination versus the horizontality of comradeship. The most powerful single image of this socio-spatial conflict occurs when Buxton arrives at the Folk Museum. Vertically, the hated Minister who had ordered the attack on the Pontyrhiw depot in which Gareth Powell was killed descends by helicopter into the car park. Horizontally and simultaneously, the crowd of enraged demonstrators surges backwards and forwards against police lines.

This spatial pattern then holds good for the rest of the novel. Its very opening sentence marks Redfern's leap into the dimension of verticality — "I was in the air fifty minutes after Buxton was shot" (5) — though neither he nor anyone else in the book succeeds in being as 'vertical' as Insatel's satellites, those "tin gods of the open sky" which silently orbit earth through the whole action (154). As he arrives in St Fagan's Norman castle, he at once ascends to the great terrace and achieves a panoptic gaze of spatial power akin to that of the former Lords of the March; he has a minor version of the same experience in Mark Evans's office, when it proves "strange to be on that kind of level with trees, staring on equal terms into their upper branches" (136). Power seems to be uneasy with horizontal space. It is precisely when Buxton and his party take a stroll in the museum grounds that he gets shot (by someone who, as a student, used to be a hurdler and is thus capable of a usurping leap upwards into his own vertical dimension), and the police, next day, seem to have equally little sense of how to handle horizontal space; 'measuring', reflects Redfern dismissively, "as the response to every disturbance" (27). But, equally, characters on the Left or from the local Welsh community become vulnerable once they enter power's own spatial axis. Gareth Powell, master of horizontality, of "the speed, the skills, the quick momentary initiatives of scrambling" (41), is shot dead precisely after clambering *up* into the army lorry. Against all this, we need to set the novel's images of a 'good' horizontality: the crowd's surges, the workers' defence of the depot, and above all Lewis Redfern's late night sprint with Rosa across Finsbury Park.

In a novel in which it politically matters so much whether you're horizontal or vertical, on the ground or up in the air, the technology for shuttling you between these two dimensions assumes an unwonted importance; and we might therefore claim that stairways and elevators are the true heroes and villains of *The Volunteers*. Gaston Bachelard maintains that "the height of city buildings is a purely exterior one. Elevators do away with the heroism of stair climbing so that there is no longer any virtue in living up near the sky" (*PS*, 27). Stairs, by contrast, turn the experience of ascent into a muscular, kinetic one, giving verticality some of the creaturely qualities of horizontal movement; there is thus, Bachelard contends, an 'oneirism' or unconscious poetry of stairs, but none of elevators. *The Volunteers* seems to bear this out. At the start of the novel Redfern has abandoned his militant past for his job with Insatel, becoming a cynical but willing agent of power and verticality; he also regularly takes the elevator to his apartment, an ascent whose social meaning he almost grasps while on board a plane to Ireland, "looking out . . . at the glitter of the sea; flying away from where the decisive events have happened" (99). When he first becomes more than professionally moved by the Buxton shooting, after his reading of the Gwent writers' pamphlet on the storming of the Pontyrhiw depot, he still takes lifts and elevators but can no longer remember using them; "I had no memory at all of leaving my room and coming down in the lift" (52). Later, as he gravitates towards Mark Evans and his secret group of Volunteers, now threatened with exposure by the media and security forces, his elevators are less efficient and head down rather than up. Setting off to burn Evans's papers, the two men take "a service lift . . . It made its slow way down" (177). But at the crucial moment of commitment, when he passes the warning to Evans, Redfern bears out Bachelard's prediction as he ascends to the office: "I went up by the stairs; the lift wasn't working" (160); and these are stairs which have an oneiric as well as pragmatic aspect, since several pages later "I was still, in my mind, with Mark Evans on the stairs" (165).

The Volunteers does, in a modest way, propose one fantasy resolution to the conflicts of vertical and horizontal space. In a novel full of conspiracies and counter-conspiracies, spaces of secrecy become paramount. The Welsh 'network' in which Lewis conceals himself before presenting his evidence against Buxton at the Pontyrhiw Inquiry seems one such space, though the terrorist David Evans notes "how open and penetrable, open and penetrated, their place really is" (191). Mark Evans, whose

Volunteers prefer slow political 'permeation' to his son's direct terrorist actions, handles secret space better, with a semi-secret room off his main business office and an adroit knack of producing clandestine documents from hidden nooks and corners of his furniture. Lewis Redfern fails dismally in this respect, locking himself away in his flat only to discover later that David Evans can effortlessly break into it, putting his personal lock on the Insatel freight bag only to find that his editor breaks it. But the most secret of spaces in this novel is a metaphorical rather than literal one, as the Williams nest crops up again. As Mark Evans frantically disposes of his papers, those secrets that Insatel will so soon expose, his wife remarks that writers are "so centered on paper they build hoards of it around them. Or like those wasps that make nests out of paper, with just a small hole to get in and out" (174). At which point we grasp why the nest is so crucial to Williams's spatial imagination (we shall see it reappear again). As a space of intimacy and protection, it is satisfyingly 'horizontal', but as an aerial space it also pertains to the dimension of verticality; it cannot, that is, be overlooked (in fantasy, at least) by the panoptic, vertical eye of power, so its secrets are safe, its locks unbroken. The nest itself looks down on roofs, as did Arthur Dean, but in a non-domineering manner; it transforms even verticality into a good, comradely 'horizontal' mode, just as the Bachelardian staircase does, though in the other direction. Unlike *Second Generation, The Volunteers* cannot actually produce the nest, but it none the less continues to haunt Raymond Williams's fiction.

The vertical eye of power is not, however, the only eye in the novel; for Lewis Redfern is a species of 'private eye' or, to put the point generically, *The Volunteers* is effectively a form of detective fiction. Though *The Fight for Manod* also contains detective elements, in Matthew and Peter's attempts to trace the sources of a series of secret speculative land deals in the Afren valley, these are only one among the rich series of forms compacted together in this 'limit-text': apocalypse, Gothic, realism, utopia, nuclear fiction. *The Volunteers*, on the other hand, seems to be a detective novel pure and simple, deeply devoted to Roland Barthes's 'hermeneutic code' (the solution of narrative mysteries): its key enigma — who shot Buxton? who dunnit? — assails us on the opening page and compels us throughout. Redfern, as a tough, iconoclastic detective, watches the police go through their own unimaginative investigative routines, which in this case have at every point been exploited in advance by the terrorist group. In this novel, as so often in the genre, both detective and master-terrorist (David Evans) are alert semioticians, masterly decoders of signs and clues; and both also know the contents of the police semiotic manual, the well-worn, entirely predictable tracks of their processes of interpretation; for "the police, at each stage, were being carefully misdirected by their own stereotypes" (64). This hard-nosed contempt for the police is only one aspect of Redfern's "corrosive scepticism", which is vividly rendered in the first-person narrative of *The Volunteers*. Its very language and syntax are curt, staccato, slangy, aggressive, the classical style of the tough, unemotional private eye. "I kept it professional", remarks Redfern (53), and indeed he does for most of the book. The depiction of him as detective then takes its place as one instance of a very general assault on the notion of 'professionalism' in Raymond Williams's work, that ethos of cool, expert, uninvolved distance from the suffering and struggles of others. This ethos comes through above all, he once argued, in television serials *about* professionals — notably doctors and policemen with, in Williams's pungent phrase, "other people as sickness or crime" (*RWT*, 103).

Every reader of *The Volunteers* can testify to its power and pace as a detective thriller. In one sense, Williams's choice of the form can itself be seen as a postmodernist move, as an instance of that aesthetic populism which seeks to break down the old dichotomy of high art/mass culture. But in another sense this particular popular genre can be counterposed to postmodernism, since detective fiction has so often been seen as a distinctly modernist form. Williams himself discusses it as co-terminous with modernism: "The detective story is an odd cultural phenomenon in itself. As a popular form it dates from that critical period of transition in the 1890s, which literary historians see as the emergence of Modernism but which cultural historians are bound to see as the stabilisation of modern middle-class forms" (*RWT*, 70). More recently, in his *Postmodernist Fiction* (1987), Brian McHale has argued for a stronger connection. He claims that modernism is a "poetics of the epistemological dominant" because its key formal and thematic concerns revolve around *knowing*: what can I know? how can I know? how can I be sure that what I think I know is actually true rather than my subjective projection onto the world? Postmodernist fiction, in McHale's view, involves a shift to a "poetics of the ontological dominant". Formally and thematically, it addresses "problems of *modes of being*", asking "What is a world? What kinds of world are there, how are they constituted, and how do they differ?; What happens when different kinds of world are placed in confrontation, or when boundaries between worlds are violated?" (*PF*, 10). The detective story, with its devotion to the question "how can I know who did it?", is thus "the epistemological genre *par excellence*", the mass-cultural double of high modernism (9). Postmodernism too, in McHale's view, has a popular counterpart, science fiction, with its construction of alternative worlds; he describes it as "the ontological genre *par excellence*" (59).

How, then, can *The Volunteers* be both detective fiction and postmodernist novel? The answer, surely, is that in it Raymond Williams impressively reworks the detective form in a postmodern direction to the point where we can see, retrospectively, that in fact all of his fiction is devoted to a "poetics of the ontological dominant". That *The Volunteers* is not classical 'modernist' detective fiction can be brought out in several ways. First because even the key epistemological mystery — who shot Buxton? — is not in the end very important. The central question the novel points us towards is: how is the terrorist attack on Buxton in the Folk Museum related to the army's killing of Gareth Powell as it stormed the Pontyrhiw power depot earlier in the year? And the right kind of answer to this question is not the detective's technical one but a cultural and political response. But, second, because in *The Volunteers* the detective ends up on the side of the criminals, helping Mark Evans burn his papers and withholding information from the police on the attack on Buxton by his son's terrorist group. In a sense, Williams is finely exploiting a paradox always latent in the genre; for if the detective is so semiotically gifted, if he can indeed spot and decipher the least clue or sign, does he not almost inhabit the criminal mentality from the inside? Is he not — to push the point a bit further — virtually a criminal himself? Traditional detective fiction can acknowledge the paradox only obliquely, when its master-criminal turns out to be more or less a double of the master-sleuth himself (Holmes and Moriarty). But in *The Volunteers* this strange logic is made explicit, and as he finally confronts the terrorists Redfern acknowledges that "it was their kind of harshness, I had always known, that I had turned, displaced to my craft" (173). Instead of any of the 'criminals' ending up in the dock, in this novel the detective does, when Redfern presents the leaked Cabinet papers revealing that Buxton had ordered the military assault to the Pontyrhiw Inquiry: "I kept getting the feeling that I was literally being taken to court; that I was in a kind of custody" (198).

The question in the long run is not epistemological — who dunnit? — but ontological: which *world* are you in, Insatel's or the Welsh workers'? It will not have escaped the reader how closely Brian McHale's ontological poetics gets to the very core of Raymond Williams's fiction: "what happens when different kinds of world are placed in confrontation, or when boundaries between worlds are crossed?". Here, precisely, is a concern with borders deeply akin to Williams's own; and it is in such ontological terms, of a crossing of frontiers between worlds, that his novels most often formulate their project. "What should I come back to?" Will asks Eira in *Border Country*: "To your own world, Will. Bringing your other world with you" (*BC*, 274). The second sentence of *Second Generation* announces that, if you stand in Between Towns Road, "you see different worlds, but there is no frontier between them" (*SG*, 9). In *The Fight for Manod* ontological terminology multiplies: Matthew Price's task as consultant is to take "with you, in yourself, the two worlds you belong in" (*FM*, 14); he stares out of his window at dawn wondering "what world would come out of these shadows, what new world" (20), and later explains to Susan "how the worlds connect. How the border got crossed" (132). In *People of the Black Mountains* the old Measurer, Dal Mered, returns to the village of his birth: "it was as if he had moved in eleven days' walk from one time, one world, to another" (*PBM*, I, 158). Such formulations, clearly, are not 'epistemological' in the modernist or detective sense, though they may on occasion entail some preliminary epistemological work (Peter Owen in *Manod* tracking down the land deals in Companies House). The epistemological quest, we might say, is essentially historical, working patiently back from the dispersed clues and signs available in the present to an origin, an earlier moment of plenitude: either the commission of the murder itself or, in high modernism, the Proustian *temps perdu* or lost time that all your *recherche* has been devoted to. But the postmodern, ontological task is essentially *spatial*, mapping the inner contours of separate worlds and then, with more difficulty, sketching a cartography of their interaction. Lewis Redfern, as I've noted, defines himself as a map-maker, and the novel maps his trajectory from the paranational world of Insatel to that of the Pontyrhiw Inquiry, pushing the detective novel via the neat device of detective-become-criminal decisively towards an 'ontological poetics'.

The case for *The Volunteers* as a postmodernist novel is strengthened by reading both it and *Manod* in the light of contemporary theories of the 'sublime', that old term from Romantic poetics which has so unexpectedly resurfaced in today's debates on postmodernism. I want to distinguish two kinds of sublime moment in postmodernism. Both are intense epiphanies of awe and even terror, but the first of them, described by Frederic Jameson as the "hysterical sublime", tends towards despair, and the second, theorised by Jean-François Lyotard, seems tentatively to point towards some kind of political hope. Jameson gives us a vivid description of the "hysterical" or what he later calls "technological sublime", and the fact that it occurs in a museum hardly seems an accident in view of the Welsh Folk Museum of *The Volunteers*:

> the ultimate contemporary fetishisation of the human body, however, takes a very different direction in the statues of Duane Hanson — what I have already called the simulacrum, whose peculiar function lies in what Sartre would have called the *derealisation* of the whole surrounding world of everyday reality. Your moment of doubt and hesitation as to the breath and warmth of these polyester figures, in other words, tends to return upon the real human beings moving about you in the museum, and to transform them also for the briefest instant into so many dead and flesh-coloured simulacra in their own right. The world thereby momentarily loses its depth and threatens to become a glossy skin, a stereoscopic illusion, a rush of filmic images without density. ('PCL', 77)

A further example that is worth invoking here is Ridley Scott's film *Blade Runner* (1982), a text whose parallels with *The Volunteers* would be worth exploring in some depth, though I shall only sketch them. It too concerns a hard-boiled, cynical detective, the 'blade runner' Deckard, whose task it is to hunt down and destroy (because once more a plodding police force is unequal to the task) a group of mutinous androids or 'replicants'. In a loose sense, these replicants are the equivalent of the political opposition in *The Volunteers*, and though Deckard does not formally align himself with them, as Redfern does with the opposition he faces, the blade runner does begin a sexual relationship with one android and his life is saved by another, their leader Roy; certainly he seems in many ways closer to the androids than to the forces of law and order he so reluctantly serves. The moment of the Jamesonian sublime, the sudden transformation of the organic into the inorganic, comes when Deckard discovers that Rachel, the attractive, sophisticated career woman who works for the Tyrone Corporation, is in fact a replicant, a robot 'more human than human' as the Tyrone slogan has it. Rachel initially does not know this, and the film later shows her bitterly trying to digest the fact that her 'human' identity — memories of girlhood, photographs of her sitting on her mother's knee — has from the start been programmed into her by the multinational corporation. Far from being an autonomous actor in her own right, she is simply the product or 'bearer' (to use a term that comes up several times in *The Volunteers*) of an alien structure. Every action she performs apparently in her own interests in fact serves its interests; she is 'written' by a script over which she has no control or even consciousness. An even more alarming moment in the film is when Rachel rounds angrily upon Deckard and asks whether he has ever taken his own computer test for replicants. This, too, is a vertiginous sublime instant; for what, we inevitably ask ourselves in fear and awe, if he took it and *did* fail? Are there *any* real human beings left in this world, and what does 'real' mean here? It is as if Juliet Dance, in *Manod*, had actually realised that she was nothing but the imitation of an imitation, a simulacrum.

Deckard doesn't take the test; Lewis Redfern does, and fails. For in Williams's novels, too, there are desolating episodes of a postmodern technological sublime, when you dimly grasp that your own deepest inner impulses may be no more than effects or stratagems of the very system you set out to oppose, that your enemy has written in advance the script that you thought was uniquely your own, that, in short, you too are a replicant, inorganic, a mere copy of a copy. One such nightmare epiphany occurs in *The Volunteers* when Redfern's investigative acumen, which he regards as a politically neutral, professional expertise, ultimately and quite against his will brings the full force of the security services crashing down on Mark Evans's Volunteers. Redfern is then plunged into the Jamesonian sublime, into a sense of himself as a self-deluded enemy agent, blindly programmed in what he thought was his private inner self; he must take the full shattering weight of a "perception of society, of my own society and of myself as its willing member, in which energy, intelligence, professional skills — all the virtues we are trained to — are so thoroughly enlisted in relationships which, at almost every level, involve calculation, indirection, half-truth, advantage" (*V*, 187). Matthew Price suffers an equally disastrous insight in *Manod* when, appalled, he sees that the very local human forces that you might hope to mobilise against multinational capital already operate within it, indeed in a strong sense are it. "This is the system", he cries, distraught, "it's become so central, so decisive, that to follow what seem our own interests, as those farmers were doing in Manod, isn't against it but is part of it; is its local reproduction" (*FM*, 153). It isn't only Juliet Dance who is a porcelain simulacrum but all the hill farmers too, because "the transactions reach right down to them. Not just as a force from outside but as a force they've engaged with, are now part of. Yet still a force that cares nothing about them" (153). This is, clearly, a deeply apolitical sublime, striking us into awed passivity through a sense that any resistance — Redfern's investigations, Price's hopes for a utopian city — is always incorporated from the start, that it is licensed by the system and merely helps it regulate itself better, that we're replicants one and all.

It's against the political despair and self-disarming that lie this way that Williams's novels evoke a second kind of postmodernist sublime, a 'good' or Lyotardian version. In *The Postmodern Condition*, Jean-François Lyotard defines his sublime moment in terms that closely follow those of the philosopher Immanuel Kant, as involving an insoluble tension between 'imagination' or what we can intellectually conceive and 'presentation' or what we can experience through our senses. In the sublime, he argues, we endure "both pleasure and pain. Better still, in it pleasure derives from pain":

> this contradiction, which some would call neurosis or masochism, develops as a conflict between the faculties of a subject, the faculty to conceive of something and the faculty to 'present' something . . . It takes place . . . when the imagination fails to present an object which might, if only in principle, come to match a concept. We have the Idea of the world (the totality of what is), but we do not have the capacity to show an example of it (*PC*, 78).

The task of avantgarde art, for Lyotard, is "to present the fact that the unpresentable exists", and since by definition it can never do this directly, it must "invent allusions to the conceivable which cannot be presented" (81) or strive for a "negative presentation" of such powerful, even utopian, ideas as the totality of all that is or "the simple (that which cannot be broken down, decomposed)" (78).

It is exactly this intertwining of pleasure and pain that seems to me to form the deepest political and aesthetic content of *The Fight for Manod* and *The Volunteers*. The pain, in the first of these novels, is evident enough. Any real assembling of political forces seems virtually hopeless at the end of the book: the Welsh farmers are deeply enmeshed in multinational manipulations, the Welsh nationalists we encounter are marginal, shadowy figures, and the frail alliance of Price and Owen, father and son, has irreparably broken down. Even the desired postmodern city is more absent from the text than I have so far made it seem. 'Manod' is real enough as a multinational plan, but the utopian postmodern opportunity that inhabits this is so radically elusive, so 'unpresentable' in Lyotard's terms, so truly one of Italo Calvino's 'invisible cities', that it nearly kills Matthew Price to hold open the space of its possibility. The novel can 'conceive' the utopian city, but it cannot 'present' it; it possesses its Idea, but cannot find an object that incarnates it. Yet it goes on doggedly striving to do so, in those remarkable, sublime moments of intensely active waiting in this novel, a simultaneously painful-pleasurable effort to will the unpresentable into being, as if the postmodern city might already inhabit the land, unseen, unknown. It is in this light that we should return to a crucial passage I have already drawn attention to, when "now there were only these growing outlines of shadow, in a world as yet without detail, without colour. What he saw in this country, which he believed he knew, was very deeply unfamiliar, a waiting strangeness, as if it was not yet known what world would come out of these shadows, what new world, that begins everyday" (*FM*, 20). Whether the final upshot of such sentences for the reader is pleasurable or painful seems impossible to say; for here the Gothic, passing through the postmodern sublime, teeters on the very brink of utopia.

The key instance of the 'good' sublime in *The Volunteers* (it is, indeed, the very conclusion of the novel) concerns 'totality' in precisely the sense that Jean-François Lyotard describes it. It constitutes nothing less, in fact, than an attempt, in a single blinding instant, to map the totality of postmodern, multinational space and the vast, unending, bafflingly tangled web of political struggles that take place within it. We might be able abstractly to 'conceive' the totality of such a global process, but we shall not, certainly, be able to 'present' it, to find a sensory object or experience that encapsulates the whole of it; as *Manod* tells us, in a passage I quoted at the start of this chapter, there is "no route in the senses" from concept to presentation. Yet Williams's novels will not simply allow the tension between the two to collapse; in their sublime moments, they strive persistently to present that awesomely 'unpresentable' political totality. As Lewis Redfern goes into the courtroom at the end of *The Volunteers* we sense that 'other dimension' which also charged much of the strangest and most moving writing in *The Fight for Manod*. He undergoes "a physical condition: as of an intense otherness, an intense possession by others. My ordinary self seemed no more than a bearer" (*V*, 199). So far this is ambivalent, hovering indeterminately between good and bad sublimes, and he could well be on the verge of discovering that he is a replicant again. However, the changing of aesthetic gears that we feel here culminates in a powerful experience of the Lyotardian postmodernist sublime, in lines which come as close as any novelist could to mapping out the impossible nature of postmodern, multinational space itself:

> To be there and to be telling it was a local moment, a significant moment, but the immense process continued and there was no available identity outside it: only the process itself, which could never be properly told in any single dimension or any single place.

There was only, now, the deep need to connect and the practical impossibility, for unregrettable reasons, of making the connections, even the known connections. Yet then, all the time, within this impossibility, were the inevitable commitments, the necessary commitments, the choosing of sides. Through the persistent uncertainty, within the overwhelming process, I had now chosen and been chosen, in what would be, in effect, a quite final way (207).

It is on such passages, as they reach stubbornly out towards impossible totalities and seek indefatigably to map perhaps ultimately unmappable surfaces, that I am content to rest my case for Raymond Williams as postmodern novelist.

An Ease of the Place: *Loyalties* and *People of the Black Mountains*

I argued in my first chapter that Raymond Williams's novels have too often been discussed as mere instances of his general social thinking, and I have aimed, against this emphasis, to explore what might at first sight seem the 'bypaths' of these texts, to trace through what Terry Eagleton terms "recurrent images, formative fantasies, intensities of feeling" at work in them. In this way, we come to grasp the textual intricacy and strangeness of these novels, everything in them which exceeds their function as neat illustrations of general social argument. But I have also suggested that these textual complexities and perplexities do not, in the long run, lead away from the social after all. Rather, they provide the basis for a new assessment of Williams's cultural thinking, at that very point where a 'postmodern novelist', meditating intently upon place, space, mapping and the socio-spatial dialectic, broadens out into a 'postmodern geographer'.

The 'margins' of Williams's novels, then, have been consistently neglected, but some commentators have gone further, not just ignoring the rich textual life of the fiction but actively arguing that there simply isn't any there at all. The novels, on this showing, are indeed 'social', but whereas most critics have said this approvingly, it now becomes a form of attack: 'social' in the sense of abstract, skeletal, schematic. Discussing *Loyalties* (1985) with its author, Michael Ignatieff proposes exactly this: "a cruel judgement of the novel would be that all of the actors are tremendously compelling representatives of historical and political movements, but very rarely do they live as psychological characters, whose motives as psychological creatures one understands" (ICA Video). The remark is made as Williams and Ignatieff debate the social issues so vividly thrown up by *Loyalties*: the relations of left-wing Cambridge intellectuals and Welsh mining families in the 1930s and beyond; the nature of the Communist Party and its relation to post-war British politics; the dilemmas of 'loyalty' faced by the Cambridge graduate Norman Braose who in later life passes technological secrets from his work in advanced computer design to the Russians, and by Gwyn Lewis, who must somehow settle the conflicting claims upon him of Braose, his natural father, and Bert Lewis, the Welsh miner who has married his mother Nesta Pritchard and brought him up.

In the interview with Ignatieff, Williams eventually concedes the criticism that has been made, "I take your general point"; and I therefore want to put to work the mode of reading, the 'postmodern spatial poetics', I have been using in this book to redeem *Loyalties* not only from Michael Ignatieff's "cruel judgement" but also from its own author's relative acquiescence in it. But then this is precisely the point of a systematic attention to the bypaths and margins of Raymond Williams's fiction. Excavating a subtext of which the author himself may be far from conscious, we can locate depths in this text — psychological, generic, spatial — which in their human consequences are considerably 'crueller' than the bland claim that they do not exist. "Would they did not!" we might imagine the novel exclaiming, so bleak is the subtextual tale it has to tell.

A remark in the interview gives us a start, pointing us towards aspects of the text the author himself cannot fully focus. Discussing Nesta, Braose's early love and Gwyn's mother, Williams refers to her as "a character I'm still not sure I understand". But why not? One answer, surely, is that a deep Williams spatial fantasy attaches to her very name; the nest which was a real object in *Second Generation* and a metaphor in *Loyalties* has now become a character in its own right. On its opening page the novel alerts us to the possibility of "puns on your name" (*L*, 4), and it heavily foregrounds Nesta's name when it first appears; Braose's sister Emma remarks, "Is it Welsh? . . . It's very unusual . . . I suppose it's just the odd associations" (21). Names in *Loyalties* are regularly charged with a weight of historical association and local legend. Norman Braose's first and second names take us right back to Matthew Price's country history in *Border Country*: "That there is a Norman roodscreen and an ancient camp and the bloodiest of the border castles and the Stone of Treachery and the gown of the reputed mistress of Robin de Braose" (*BC* 69), a history whose archetypes haunt the politics of the mid-twentieth century.

If the one real, human-size nest in Williams turns up in the context of the relationship of Kate Owen and Arthur Dean, it is perhaps not surprising that this echo of it — the name rather than the thing itself — turns up in the context of Nesta and Norman Braose's love. For this is an exact structural equivalent of the earlier pairing: a working-class woman whose talents (painting in Nesta's case) find little outlet in her home community turns in frustration to an intellectual whose love, though initially based on recognition of that exceptional talent, has no enduring basis. Ultimately, the nearest Nesta gets to Kate's nest is a cobweb one: "There was a very old stone font beyond the door. Nesta lifted the lid and looked inside. It was dry, with cobwebs" (36). But an imagery of birds, eggs and nests, of vegetation writhing and wreathing itself as if striving to become a nest, thereafter pervades the novel: the garlands and clusters carved on the roodscreen in the church, the intricate patterning of ferns in Monkey Pitter's carpet, the overgrown riverbank that so attracts Braose in Oxford, or the "thick undergrowth of bramble" that Gwyn pushes through in the grounds of Braose's country house. War, too, is oddly tied in to an imagery of birds and nests, as in the anti-Vietnam war painting of a "huge and distorted bird flying above and overshadowing a tangle of leaves and flowers . . . the tangle of branches", a bird which seems to cancel out the very possibility of the nest (213). Fighting in Spain in 1937, Bert Lewis momentarily finds a nest-like security in the "shelter of a gorse-bush on the lip of a hollow" (51); and in some oblique way nests even feature in the Normandy tank battle in which Bert is badly injured for, as he speculates, the German tank crew "probably only went into the farm for some eggs": "if the bloody chickens make off, there'll still be eggs" — and nests too, presumably (85). The binoculars which become so central a symbol in the novel first enter the narrative when Paul Howe offers Bert "a look at some bird he had spotted" (54).

The Williams nest is thus scattered and diffused across this text, failing to constitute itself in any full sense because the fundamental spatial imagination of *Loyalties* is not Bachelardian topophilia but, rather, a space of terror and incarceration. Nesta, being a gifted amateur artist, first succeeds in sombrely defining this space. As she and Norman listen to a political lecture in the barn in 1937, she sketches busily:

> an extension of the dark vaulted shape of the barn, with its heavy stone walls and its narrow openings like arrowslits. It was now as much a castle as a barn, but seen from inside, as if by a prisoner. There was only one beam of light, from a small high window, and there were no people illuminated by it, only a strongly drawn and elongated hand, almost skeletal across the diffusing light (23).

"We're through the Gothic line", remarks Emma in 1944 as she consults Bert Lewis's war maps (98); and indeed we are. For *Loyalties* systematically uses painting as Charlotte Brontë does at the start of *Jane Eyre*, to convey intensities of psychic pain and desire which can never rise fully into consciousness; and one of the most harrowing moments in the novel is when Nesta finally shows Gwyn her long-hidden portraits of the young Braose and the wounded Bert. Perhaps the characters in the novel are, as Michael Ignatieff suggests, a little too politically articulate; but then the novel finds means, through the device of Nesta's painting, to express their unconscious, and indeed to unleash its own unconscious through that "wall papered with faces" that Williams had contemplated with a fascinated horror in 'Drama in a Dramatized Society'. It is along these lines that he might have replied to Ignatieff's critique, though symptomatically the paintings never once enter their discussion of *Loyalties*.

This Gothic space of terror, enclosure and entrapment dominates the novel, and tears the counter-vailing impulse towards the nest(a) into the dispersed shreds I have reconstructed above. The most horrific image of Gothic space here is the wartime experience of the tank, that formidable metal enclosure which offers so little chance of escape when itself attacked. Nesta's sketch seems to become literal as Bert discovers "a corpse burned to an almost shapeless blackness . . . under the engine cowling. Another body, still retaining some of its shape, hung halfway out of the turret" (91) — a trauma which returns to afflict Bert as he dies. But carceral space reaches well beyond this into the text: politically, with the demonstrators in Grosvenor Square in 1968 crushed between police lines and their own fellow marchers in the rear, or in the Welsh experience of the 1984 miners strike, in "this township that

seemed now under siege" (330); technologically, in a fascination
with cramped underground space, embodied partly in the labour of
the miners but also in Gwyn's work drilling the ocean bed for
possible nuclear waste disposal sites; and finally in terms of
espionage itself, in those *inner* carceral spaces into which Monkey
Pitter and Norman Braose have stashed away the secret of their
work for the Russians, inner spaces which draw the whole man
back into them, so that Braose becomes "a wraith. The
disturbance, the passion, the beliefs of any kind, shrivelled inside
him" (320).

In Gothic space, what else would one expect to find but the
Gothic body, a body to inspire horror and loathing? And *Loyalties*
is indeed full of mutilated, deformed or just freakish bodies. The
first notable instance is Monkey Pitter, who even at the age of thirty
is on his way to becoming a grotesque: "the spectacles were heavier
and the thicker lenses seemed to clench and wither the small ugly
features. He now stooped more also" (104). He arouses an
impressive revulsion in others, as when Braose's wife reacts to his
name with a violent "immediate physical reaction" or an American
airman looks at him "with an evident but probably physical
contempt" (173, 105). Such disgust is partly a response to his
homosexuality, but if we take seriously the "puns on your name"
with which *Loyalties* opens, other possibilities present themselves.
Catching the details of Gwyn's brother's fine in a garbled telephone
conversation, his wife reports that "it sounded like it was paid by a
monkey" (230); and in a novel in which evolutionary theory is
several times discussed, Monkey's physical peculiarities, which
accelerate as he grows older, come to have the air of some
Darwinian throwback, as if he were a missing link which had never
quite made it to full humanity and were now busy regressing back
up the evolutionary path towards apehood. This, at any rate, seems
to be the theory to which he himself inclines; for on the door of his
London flat "the big brass knocker was shaped to an ape's face"
(312). Monkey's sub-body is well complemented by the hyper-
body of Emma Braose's son, Bill, "Six six and a half . . . And yes it
does cause problems" (232).

But the most ghastly body of all in *Loyalties* is that of Bert Lewis,
who suffers dire injuries during the tank battle in Normandy:
"across his face a flame that was more like light than touch or

immediate hurt . . . a sudden hammerblow on his right knee" (93). With the ensuing permanent limp and severe mutilation of one side of his face, Lewis acquires in a single gesture the two modes of physical damage that most torment Raymond Williams's fiction. The damage to Ivor Vaughan's leg in *Manod* and the shooting of Buxton in the legs in *The Volunteers* both carry a castration fantasy, as does Bert's wounded leg here; even Gwyn, as a toddler, is "slow to walk", as if sharing in his adopted father's disability (118). Damage to faces had already featured in *Manod*, in the form of Gwen's disfiguring red blotches, and becomes a major issue in *Loyalties*. Fighting in Spain, Bert realises that "always, it seemed, the first move was to protect the face" (60); and thirty years later a controversy breaks out over whether the burnt ashes of a Whip's notice that Alec Merritt flings into the face of a Labour Foreign Secretary were or were not still burning: "I wouldn't have minded if it was. It might have given him some idea of napalm" (215). We also come across a sinister faceless face or anti-face, which is this novel's equivalent of *Border Country*'s room-which-was-not-a-room, in a London art gallery: "an extraordinary drawing he could now see, in which the head seen from the side was like a rock slab, almost without features" (214).

The wartime damage to Bert's face is not a static mutilation. It worsens as the years pass and, more importantly, lives on as active process in the painting of the wounded Bert that Nesta does in 1944 and which she at last shows to Gwyn forty years later.

> It was immediately Bert: the face was never in doubt. The oils were streaked and jabbed to the domination of the jagged eye: hard pitted lines of grey and silver and purple pulling down the staring dark socket. The whole face, under the cropped hair, was distorted around these lines which pulled from the dark hollow. Angry streaks of crimson and purple pulled beyond the hard shoulder. . . It was terrible beyond any likeness, as if the already damaged face was still being broken and pulled apart, as all the lines seemed to move (346).

Gothic space here is, so to speak, centrifugal rather than centripetal as it was in Nesta's sketch of the barn, a violent dismembering of a human centre rather than its intensive spatial compression. Bert's portrait has its full significance only in contrast with Nesta's earlier painting of Norman Braose, a portrait Gwyn describes as "more than happy. It's a great burst of sunlight and sky" (345). And with these two powerful pictures side by side, we enter a realm which is certainly one of conscious political choice for Gwyn but is also, in an uncanny way, 'psychological'. In their ICA conversation, Ignatieff and Williams discuss the former at length, but remain entirely silent on the latter; yet the whole point of *Loyalties*, it seems to me, is that these two dimensions are inseparable. The Cambridge Left intellectuals betray the very working class in whose name they act: sexually, as Braose does Nesta, and politically, in their slavish adherence to a foreign power rather than to a native socialism. Yet despite this betrayal, the lives of that class, of Bert and Nesta say, remain honourable and courageous ones, whereas the Cambridge Communists variously collapse in upon themselves as the years pass — to the point where Emma has locked herself forever away in a world of past certainties, Monkey has become some kind of recluse, and Braose, pottering about in his wood, is a "wraith", "now as before . . . unfit to relate to others" in Gwyn's damning judgement (364).

Yet a suave Cambridge social manner and style persists, even as a simple matter of physical beauty. In 1945 Braose "with his mop of bright hair, looked much as he had when he was an undergraduate" in 1937 (105); in 1956 Mark Ryder glances at him and concludes ruefully that "these are men who weather beautifully. The face was still fine-drawn and handsome, still relatively unlined" (186). Once Braose inherits the country house, Nayles, from his aunt, the epithet 'weathered' features more and more often in the text as applied to it; "this is just a house", remarks Emma cavalierly (169), but both her brother and the novel know better than that. As we saw in Chapter Two, space is not just the product of social relations, but bends back upon and actively shapes them in its turn, and the aesthetic delights of this mellow English space are the final nails (or Nayles) in the coffin of Braose's Communist convictions. Yet even so, what the country house reinforces in him is exterior style, however urbane, while within, as he testifies in rare moments of frankness, a tormenting psychic "tearing from that past" rages on and "terror then comes" (178, 358) — a psychic condition objectified by the fungus that fascinates Braose in the wood.

We cannot read the actual physical damage to Bert Lewis's face as a symbol of Braose's betrayal of his class; to do so would demean it, for it is the result of his own brave struggle against Fascism. But we can so interpret the continuing mutilation in Nesta's portrait, that perpetual breaking apart of the face at every moment of its existence. Braose remains the suave English scholar-gentleman that he always was, but the painting seems to violently age and degenerate *for* him, as if it did so 'on his behalf', becoming the objective correlative of an inner torment he is less and less able to acknowledge to himself and others. Braose is an ever more elusive figure as the novel proceeds, increasingly a topic for discussion, report, rumour or interpretation rather than an actor in his own right; but all the while Nesta's terrible portrait blazons forth the truth of his inner being. In a sense, what she unveils to Gwyn is not so much one portrait of Bert Lewis and one of Norman Braose as two of Braose, the one being mere signifier or surface and the other its signified or depth. But here *Loyalties* has rejoined that Gothic tradition which was already hovering so sinisterly around the margins of *The Fight for Manod*. For with this narrative structure — of a man all sweetness and light whose accelerating psychic degeneracy is registered secretly and repulsively only on a hidden painting — Williams has given us a latter-day, politicised version of Oscar Wilde's *The Portrait of Dorian Grey*. There are indeed, then, *pace* Michael Ignatieff, uncanny Gothic depths stirring within the grand historical themes of *Loyalties*; and we can only wonder, with *Dorian Grey* in mind, whether if Gwyn had attacked and destroyed his mother's portrait of the torn face, Norman Braose, 'Braose bradwr' in his wood at Westridge (305), would not instantly have fallen down dead.

* * *

In my discussion of *The Fight for Manod* I cited Gaston Bachelard's claim that "late in life, with indomitable courage" we say that we are going to build a house. Lest such building prove too arduous, he also offers a more modest suggestion as to how we might explore these "dreams of a house that we shall live in later, always later":

> An excellent exercise for the function of inhabiting a dream house consists in taking a train trip. Such a voyage unreels a film of

117

houses that are dreamed, accepted and refused without our ever having been tempted to stop, as we are when motoring. We are sunk deep in daydreaming with all verification healthily forbidden (*PS*, 62).

We have already seen this process at work in Raymond Williams's fiction. As Matthew Price travelled back to London in *Border Country* he looked out from the train at the English country houses on his route and then, four novels later, Williams lives his way imaginatively into just such a house, when Norman and Emma Braose inherit Nayles in Westridge. Yet the most formidable of all such Bachelardian 'train journeys' in Williams's work is his enormous final project, *People of the Black Mountains*, a vast historical novel of his native area of Wales from 23,000 B.C. to the present day, a novel planned as a trilogy but cut short by its author's death and now ending, after two volumes, in 1415 A.D. This rich work deserves and will no doubt receive many kinds of critical attention, many of which will involve a professional expertise which the present author makes no claim to possess. The range and audacity of its imaginative reconstructions of the Welsh past will invite scrutiny from anthropologists, archaeologists, etymologists, military historians and others, as well as critics with a more general concern with issues of Welsh culture and identity. Even in its unfinished state, *People of the Black Mountains* is a novel that will be preoccupying us for many years to come.

My own aim here, writing so soon after the novel's publication, is necessarily a modest and provisional one. I shall seek to trace in it, sometimes at its surface, sometimes buried at more oblique, hidden layers of the text, the motifs I have been mapping in earlier chapters, reading *People of the Black Mountains* in the context of topo-analysis and socio-spatial dialectic, as a grand exploration of technologies and fantasies of habitation, which in turn unleash some of the key Williams images and obsessions. Finally, I conclude with two generic hypotheses which dovetail with my overall account of Raymond Williams as 'postmodern novelist'. Like *Border Country*, Williams's last novel is both deeply historical and yet not one-sidedly 'historicist' in Edward Soja's usage of that term. It is, rather, the crowning demonstration in Williams of a socio-spatial dialectic, the decisive text on which to base a description of him as postmodern geographer.

As Glyn Parry sets off at night across the Black Mountains in search of his grandfather Elis, who has failed to return from an afternoon walk across them, he is briefly tempted by a vision of them as abstract Enlightenment space, by "the sense of a *tabula rasa*: an empty ground on which new shapes could move. Yet that ideal of a dissident and dislocated mind, that illusion of clearing a space for wholly new purposes, concealed, as did these mountains, old and deep traces along which lives still moved" (*PBM*, I, 11).

Tabula rasa: this, as we have seen, is the ideal of modernist architecture, which sweeps away every last trace of local history or tradition in favour of its own gleaming, rectilinear white facades. For the postmodernist, however, the local qualities of space are to be respected and reactivated, as they usually are for Glyn himself. Glancing at the eroded dugout of an ancient hut, he confesses that "he had often walked into one of these hollows and closed his eyes, trying to feel its generations of life" (12). The whole novel is then devoted to this effort of reactivation, to inhabiting the very process of inhabiting. The opening sentences of the book read: "See this layered sandstone in the short mountain grass. Place your right hand on it" (1), and this gesture of the hand closing upon stone is the fundamental experience of the body in *People of the Black Mountains*, of the body about to begin or in the midst of or having just finished building. It is repeated over and over: in the hands of Varan holding and tossing pebbles in 16,000 B.C.; in Idris and Gizon "whose hands loved stone" in 3000 B.C. (121); in the slave Karan secretly fingering a flake of sandstone during a tense encounter with Lugon in 250 B.C. Glyn recalls an "isolated, baffling, early report" about the original people of the mountains, that "from the time of their coming into the island they fell under the spell of the stones" (235); and indeed they do, naming their children after them (Kargen) and becoming known to their more powerful successors as the Old Ones or the Stone People.

The novel is devoted to this active experience of space, to a transformation of space into place through an intimate working of stone in which all the later binary oppositions of our own culture — subject/object, planner/materials — seem not to exist, since men and stones become part of an indissociable process: "the men handled and tested each stone, imagining its lie, until they were at last offered to fit together and endure" (123). But then what exactly do they build with them? At this point, we need to invoke a key principle of Bachelardian topo-analysis, for it is not simply a matter "of describing houses, or enumerating their picturesque features":

> we must go beyond the problems of description . . . in order to attain to the primary virtues, those that reveal an attachment that is native in some way to the primary function of inhabiting. A geographer or an ethnographer can give us descriptions of very varied types of dwellings. In each variety, the phenomenologist makes the effort to seize upon the germ of the essential, sure, immediate well-being it encloses. In every dwelling, even the richest, the first task of the phenomenologist is to find the original shell (*PS*, 4).

I shall therefore seek to elicit the "original shell", the founding structure of Raymond Williams's spatial imagination — a 'shell' which is common to the extraordinary variety of dwellings within these mountains across the 37,000 years of the novel's action because it is, in the last analysis, for Williams the spatial structure of these very mountains, of border country itself.

Stone People, indeed, but then building in stone is a relatively late technology; and if we look for *its* original shell, the fundamental gesture of human habitation, we shall perhaps find it in the behaviour of Manod's family during the storm in Little Stone Valley: "without shelter of any kind, unless there had been time to get to the dip slope, they would be huddled together, the women bending their heads and the children wrapped in the centre" (25). In this, the novel's first flashback to the past, original space is female space, a primal space of nurture and nesting. So too are the caves in which these ancient people live; in the second story — 16,000 rather than 23,000 B.C. — the cave is a metaphorical protective womb for Almet's literal labouring one as her baby girl is born. And so too is the Long House, the great cultural and architectural achievement of the early people. During its building, around 3000 B.C., "the younger men would have left the house at that, once the standers were in place, but the mothers were insistent that their place of living must be properly marked" (122). A thousand years later, at a mid-winter ceremony, the identification of the Long House as female space is strengthened:

> All eyes were now fixed on the body of a woman, which lay in a death fold on top of the honour stone . . . Slowly a hand rose and

its fingers extended . . . moving to a knee with a fist on the ground, then to both knees and with joined arms above the head, the body unwound and rose and stood above the honour stone. There was a long silence, and then from around the feet, seeming to escape from the Long House itself, birds were flying: a darting flutter of wrens in the fading light (186).

With the release of wrens, of course, the Long House metamorphoses into that structure which we have already seen to be so close to the Williamsite original spatial shell: the nest.

The prevalence of nest imagery in the first volume of *People of the Black Mountains* is perhaps not surprising, given the primitive building techniques of these early epochs. The hut, Bachelard argues, "appears to be the tap-root of the function of inhabiting" (*PS*, 31), and in this novel huts are clearly human nests, "just a stack of leaning branches" or, one step further on, the stack of branches with coarse heather packed between them (105–7). Marod may have been a cave-dweller, but a 'technology of nests' is important to him too, since to get a fire from his flint he must skilfully "make a nest of dry grass" (26), and throughout these early centuries nestlings are a significant part of the people's diet. In later years nests are more often metaphorical than literal: "You have carried them in triumph to your own nests", cries Tewdyr to the trapped Viking Agnar, denouncing him for making warriors into slaves (II, 145). The most prodigious of all metaphorical nests is that which gives the second volume, *The Eggs of the Eagle*, its very title: "on a certain day, on a ledge in the rockfall of Ysgyryd, where in the oldest days the giant Orgo rested his heel, a young shepherd found the nest of the Eagle. The nest was broken and deserted, but three great eggs lay within it" (II, 67). This broken nest of Mabon's vision is partly the power of Rome over the Black Mountains, which now in 420 A.D. has disintegrated, but it is also the land itself, devastated by the long invasion and occupation and resistance. 'Nest', at any rate, becomes a Welsh rather than Roman name, beginning its long historical descent to Nesta Pritchard in *Loyalties*. When we learn as Gruffydd ap Llewellyn marches on Hereford in 1055 A.D. that he has a daughter called Nest, the great battle ahead seems suddenly to be architecturally defined, a war of incompatible spaces: Welsh nest versus Norman castle. A woman named Nest features in 'Widows of the Welshry', an episode I shall return to; and our sense of the nest as a female space is reinforced by a beautiful image in 'The Gift of Acha' when Acha wades out into the river:

> Looking quickly around to make sure she was alone, she pulled the skirts of her long tunic up to her waist. As she felt cool air on her skin a kingfisher darted from the bank just below her . . . It was in some way as if she had released the lovely bird, as if it had flown from herself (II, 121).

The 'nest' now is a female pubic or genital one, that most intimate of spaces here briefly exposed to the outside world and bestowing its 'gift', its inhabitant, upon it. Again, Williams's fiction would have bolstered Gaston Bachelard's tireless "search for nests in literature", for Bachelard too quotes a writer who "had just discovered the feminine significance of a nest set in the fork of two branches" (*PS*, 96). Spaces of domination — Dal Mered's great Round House Menvandir, Roman harbours and cities, Norman castles — seek across the centuries to impose their will upon and remake in their own unlovely image the spaces of habitation; and all of the latter — caves, huts, Long Houses, the artificial island in Lake Llangorse, the grass circle that escapes the earthquake — are ultimately assimilable to the nest, their original shell. Yet since that nest is also a female one, a disturbing sexual politics of place comes into play here.

People of the Black Mountains begins and ends with a crippled male: the boy Gan who dies of exposure while Marod and his family track the herd of horses and, forty-two thousand years later, Glyn's grandfather Elis, who was to have been found "with an injured foot, inside the stone circle of Garn Wen" at the end of the third volume (II, 322). It has many more cripples between these two, including the ageing but still powerful hunter Mirin, "crippled for two winters" (I, 41), the wounded Bear hunter, "trying not to limp but with the blood running freely down his leg", whom Cara desires (I, 67), and the Measurer Dal Mered, "a bad injury; the whole foot was swollen and dark" (I, 159). Perhaps we should read little into this: in the rugged landscapes and medically backward epochs the novel narrates, such accidents are easily seen as common, and to a degree they extend to women too. Or if we do require a more general interpretation, we can turn to Claude Lévi-Strauss's account of Oedipus, whose name means 'swollen foot'. "In mythology it is a universal characteristic of men born from the earth that at the moment they emerge from the depth they either cannot walk or they walk clumsily" (*SA*, 215). This theory fits neatly into the spatial schema of Williams's novel, where the 'horizontality' of the rooted natives is often contrasted with the 'verticality' of alien cultures of domination: raiders on horseback, builders of castles and towers, "while you still creep close to the earth" (I, 306).

And perhaps the best example in Williams of this chthonic, Lévi-Straussian crippling is Telemon the Finder, who "could feel with his long fingers the points of life in certain stones, so strongly that as he touched them he would be thrown to the ground" (I, 224). Yet we have also come across images of crippling in the novels where such mythic meanings are not at stake: the tractor crashing on to Ivor Vaughan's leg in *Manod*, the shooting of Buxton in the legs in *The Volunteers*, and the wounding of Bert Lewis's leg in battle in *Loyalties*. These earlier acts of crippling seemed, rather, to be related to powerful female figures in those texts: Gwen Vaughan galloping on Cavalier, Rosa Brant literally shooting Buxton, even Nesta Pritchard, who morally betrays Lewis through her sexual relations with Norman Braose. The very first, though rudimentary, instance of this motif is afforded by Bill Hybart in *Border Country* who, in the presence of his formidable wife, "stumbled a little as he moved" (*BC*, 48).

Within this context of powerful women/crippled men, let us insert one further episode of injury from *People of the Black Mountains*. The story of 'The Widows of the Welshry' is written explicitly to celebrate tough women, Mair and Nest, who remain strong and resilient under almost intolerable pressures. At the start of the episode, Ieuan rubs his hands delightedly over his wife Mair's pregnant belly, lifting "the rough woollen cloth. His fingers moved, gentle, over her warm skin" (II, 263). Three pages later he is dead, in a sudden, shocking accident that we can readily relate back to Ivor's accident in Manod:

> the waggon fell over him. As it tipped the oxen went down and the uppermost log slid forward and hit Ieuan hard on the back of the neck. He screamed as he fell. Idris had fallen in the ditch. But he could not move . . . Fighting for breath, Idris tried to release his leg (265).

That ultimate space of protection, the womb-nest, thus metamorphoses, in a few textual moments, into a familiar Williams pattern of crippling, castration and death. The accident is, as it were, presided over by the other woman in this tale, where this linked structure of protection/crippling is signalled by the disparity between her Bachelardian name and her actual aggressiveness; for Idris's wife, Nest, is "strong and determined . . . a hard woman" (282). Nest wreaks upon everyone around her a vengeful bitterness for her rape at the age of fifteen by Henry Bailey, a rape which, when tried in court, produces one of the most bizarre sexual moments in all of Williams's fiction: "they told me to hold him . . . His thing! His prick. I had to hold it in my hand, and the holy relic in the other, and say: 'with this I now hold he penetrated my body . . .' " (277). The phallic invasion of this womb-nest has thus converted that nurturing enclosure, Mair's belly, cave of caves and hut of huts, into a castrating one, a space in which Vaughan, Buxton, Lewis and Idris crash crippled to the ground. What is articulated in this recurrent motif, evidently, is a deep fear of women or, better, fear of female space or the womb-nest, a space which is, however, also intensely desired. Though this spatial ambivalence operates with particular intensity in a sexual context, it is also, I believe, of general relevance to *People of the Black Mountains*, constituting nothing less than the 'original shell' of the text's spatial imagination. The occasional local acts of 'revenge' that men in Williams's novels achieve in this context of sexually motivated crippling, as in that odd episode in *Loyalties* when a policeman stamps on the foot of a woman demonstrator in Grosvenor Square, or when the girl Pani has bitterly to accept her deflowering by the ageing cripple Mirin in *People of the Black Mountains*, are momentary resolutions of a spatial tension which can never finally be settled.

To speak of the 'original shell', however, is perhaps too static an image. For what is central to the spatial poetics of Williams's last novel is process and transformation, a swift or slow metamorphosis whereby organic space becomes dead space, the womb-nest transmuting into a Gothic zone of horror and death. Local instances include the charcoal pile whose construction fascinates the giant Tami in Grain Valley, an enclosed combustion which renders down living substance into the inorganic as thoroughly as did the burning tank in *Loyalties*, and the diseased hive which

Caran opens before Lord Morudd: "A mass of blackened wax and dead bees fell to the grass. 'Great Gods, what a stench!' " (II, 76). More substantial human examples are the stone circle which Carvor marks as a place of safety from earthquake in 1600 B.C. but which during the anthrax epidemic a century later becomes a space of horror and pestilence, "a stinking huddle of death" (I, 233); the artificial island built in Lake Llangorse, that protective container which turns into a lethal trap the moment Agnar and his Vikings invade it; and the great hall of William de Braose's castle, whose measured ceremonies and good cheer mutate in an instant into massacre.

These local spatial metamorphoses operate in this novel under the sign of the Gothic, which here, as in *Loyalties*, is a matter of shattered or mutilated faces. The link passages of *People of the Black Mountains*, which consist of Glyn's meditations as he tramps across the mountains searching for his grandfather, are so impressively packed with historical information and metahistorical reflection that we tend to forget, looking back, that this layer of the text too began in terror. In the darkness on the far side of a gulley Glyn makes out "the low mound of a stone-age grave. He turned away from it, suddenly chilled" (II, 11); and so he should turn away, since this grave at once releases its inhabitants, its long dead who are also *un*dead: "he kept swinging round, as if somebody was close to him . . . The sense of a close presence had come again and alarmed him" (12–13). In a nearly literal sense, the boy becomes a medium through which the spirits of the ancient dead ventriloquise their long sufferings and briefer joys. Elements of Gothic then appear memorably in the body of the text itself. The vast historical sweep of this novel is not only an exploratory Bachelardian train journey, but also allows a generic flexibility inhibited in Williams's more 'realist' contemporary fiction. The hints towards apocalypse in *The Fight for Manod* here become the full-blown thing itself, as in that vivid, distraught episode of 'The Black Stranger and the Golden Ram', in which anthrax arrives in these mountains around 1450 B.C. and devastates their sheep and people; "by midwinter the whole way of life of the mountains had been almost destroyed" (I, 231).

When the Black Stranger arrives with his deadly ram young Telim stares closely at his face and arms: "there were strange, dark, nearly black lumps at several places on his skin" (225). We have, in short, entered the textual zone of that other key Williams motif — not the damaged leg but the disfigured *face*, the faces, say, of Gwen Vaughan and Bert Lewis. It is a motif that flits in and out of *People of the Black Mountains*, alighting on the blotched face of a drummer at Begisso in 2600 B.C. and on the young priest, Ieuan, "disfigured by red swellings" in 740 A.D. (II, 111). But its definitive appearance in this novel occurs in 'Bibra in Magnis' in 300 A.D. where the Gothic horror implicit in so many of this text's spatial metamorphoses (womb-nest to claustrophobia and death) receives expression in its raw state. For the horror of disfigurement seems, as Gwen Vaughan had already memorably suggested, to be an essentially female emanation in Williams's fiction. "With half a face you've only got half a brain", the other girls tease Bibra, and when the carter meets her years later he sees just what they mean:

> it was when she looked up at him, challenging him about the work, that the real shock had come. It was an old woman's nutcracker face . . . but something terrible had happened to it. It was as if the whole right side was not there. The right eye was dragged, the right edge of the mouth was crooked, the cheek that should have been between them had atrophied (II, 44).

It is a face which disgusts everyone who looks at it, and whose disintegration across the years, from the prettiness of the child to the hideousness of the crone, the novel traces in appalling detail. We are in the presence here, surely, of pure textual obsession. For Bibra serves no significant narrative function; she witnesses the clash between Lord Magalos and the merchant Eppius and is killed during it, but in no way illuminates the cultural conflict fought out through it. In a note to the novel, Joy Williams writes that "the body of an elderly woman, deformed in exactly the same way as Bibra, was actually found at Kentchester" (II, 326); and here, surely, was what the sexual and spatial poetics of this novel was waiting for, an actual historical peg on which to hang a horrific motif that had become ever more clamorous in the fiction since Gwen Vaughan first galloped in to it. Primal space, in *People of the Black Mountains*, is female space, that protective womb-nest which, a moment later, traps and cripples you; and the shattered half-face of the slave-woman Bibra gives undiluted expression to the primal Gothic terror aroused by that spatial trauma.

The womb-nest or 'original shell' may be incarnated in a particular woman or building, but as we come slowly to grasp over the seven hundred pages of the novel, it in the end coincides with the mountains themselves, with the border country they form. Sometimes this is literally, visually, so, when human action directly transforms the mountains into a protective container: in 550 A.D., say, when the road from Abergavenny is barricaded and then a great ring of fire is ignited around the district to keep out the plague that rages on the banks of the Severn. More often their enclosures are benevolent in a military or political sense, affording spaces of security for those who live at the margins of the social order — Derco, the hunter of Menhebog or, later, the three shepherds released from captivity in Abergavenny by a popular uprising. At rare moments characters in the novel coincide with its own spatial poetics and articulate precisely this sense of an ultimate womb-nest whose only threats are from elsewhere. Seeking in 1265 A.D. to dissuade his sons from entering military service, the former monk Conan tells them that in his youth, "sitting like this on the mountain, I had what I thought was a vision": "I looked at these mountains, and they seemed like walls to protect a sweet holiness settled among them . . . It seemed then that this whole country was given to God . . . Out there the unending struggle for power" (II, 248–9).

But even at this extended geographical level, the spatial metamorphosis I have tracked through the text still applies. The accoutrements of Gothic horror may fade into the background, belonging as they mainly do to the sexual working through of this theme, but spatial mutation still takes place. We might, indeed, regard the whole of this weighty novel as hingeing on a single pun, whereby 'inhabiting' shifts a vowel and is experienced as 'inhibiting'. This is as true of earliest times, where Marod and his family suddenly react against "the staleness of the cave" (I, 17), as it is thirty-five thousand years later when Conan's sons dismiss his geographical vision; "Are we to stay here all our lives, in this back of beyond?" (II, 237). One man's womb-nest is another man's Gothic incarceration; or, more accurately, place is always both simultaneously, walling me in even as it barricades my adversary out. The title of the second volume, *Eggs of the Eagle*, captures this exactly. Eggs are the ultimate benevolent space, their every last

127

cubic millimentre packed with nurture, but they are also of course enclosures of which the whole point is to get out, to hatch and define an autonomy of your own.

In every generation, then, a conflict is fought out between those for whom place is the ultimate value and those for whom it is a Gothic catacomb, frustrating what they see as their authentic life elsewhere. It is a conflict which takes form in the novel in certain decisive set-pieces, tense and extended debates between 'place' and a 'modernity' that offers to transcend it: conversations between the boy Karan and the Measurer Dal Mered in 2000 B.C.; the intricate disputes in 250 B.C. of the slave Karan with Lugon, Wise One to Lord Eliudon, over the death-sentence on Derco; and some of Glyn's own meditations on "Roman forms of definition . . . Romanising minds" (II, 63). Yet the two later instances are, unusually for this novel, the simpler ones, because the appeals made in them to 'space' rather than 'place', to formal universality over concrete locatedness, are clearly the rationalisations of a brutal ruling order. It is centrally in 'The Coming of the Measurer', which is certainly one of the most developed and effective episodes in the novel, that these matters are truly threshed out.

'Measuring' has been a resonant term in Raymond Williams's fiction ever since the first page of *Border Country*, and 'The Coming of the Measurer' seeks to focus the very instant in which disinterested, universalising inquiry separates itself out from pragmatic knowledge, from the calculating of midsummer, the study of animal disease, the predicting of the weather. Professional measurers such as Mered and his Great Company at Menvandir are already dependent on the division of labour; others herd, hunt and cook so that they may eat and study. Yet this is not yet exploitative, since the benefits they give back to the community in practical knowledge are their own distinctive contribution to general human welfare. Yet once their measuring becomes disinterested, a purely internal scientific pursuit, can this delicate compact be maintained? It seems not, for Menvandir has demanded ever greater exactions of food and labour from its local people, has used its knowledge of an imminent eclipse to overawe their protests, and has instituted an order of armed guards to protect its privileges. And yet through the forlorn figure of Dal Mered, returning like Matthew Price to his native village, in despair at what he has seen the educated world turn into, *People of the Black Mountains* deeply wants to hold on to a faint possibility that the degeneration of Menvandir was not inevitable after all, and that the relations between universal scientific inquiry and lived local interests need not be so starkly antagonistic. And yet all Dal Mered does is inflict upon the very community that hospitably shelters him while his leg heals the kind of structural split of which he himself was a part at Menvandir. For we learn later that the boy Karan, initially torn between his community's traditional wisdom and the Measurer's modernity, opted ultimately for the latter and became a 'Dal' or Measurer at Menvandir himself. In his bleakest moment, Mered almost knows he will have this disruptive impact on local life: "what I must now measure is that I too am of that company . . . I am against those Dalen, but I am still Dal" (I, 180). He here predicts, four thousand years in advance, the dilemma of the Cambridge Communists in *Loyalties*, and his own impact upon Karan is akin to Norman Braose's on Nesta, rudely tearing him out of the settled routines of community. Is there, Williams's fiction seems persistently to ask, something about the very nature of abstract, universalising inquiry that means that even an intellectual politically aligned with an oppressed local community will — indeed, must — betray it?

To turn from Dal Mered and Karan to the slave Karan and Lugon eighteen hundred years later is to see the question answered too easily in the affirmative. Lugon, like Mered, affirms the values of a universalism that cancels place: "There is this place or another, and in every place there is the law". Karan, speaking with "the emphasis of an older people", counters with a place-specific rationality: "in every place there are truths, wise one" (I, 303). Karan is here wholly vindicated against Lugon, whose abstractions rationalise a violent social order — an order which gruesomely executes the slave at the end of this episode, when "Lugon himself brought the strangling rope" (308); modernity is discredited, place prevails. But in the Dal Mered episode, the novel never relaxes the tension. Yes, Menvandir has become domineering, but it may *still* be the "growing point of the world". Mered belongs "to its modernity, and his mind could never slip back into these old settled ways" (158); and this is both his human limitation and a necessary refusal of the genuinely parochial elements of local custom. The

Karan-Lugon episode is simply anti-modernist or revivalist; but the Karan-Dal Mered encounter is postmodernist, never just collapsing the claims of universal reason in its reaffirmation of the values of place and tradition. The overall project of *People of the Black Mountains* is to define this most baffling of all border countries, locating itself determinedly in the fissure between prefix and noun, 'post-' and 'modernism'.

People of the Black Mountains is the second of Williams's novels to make use of a narrative framing device outside the main historical action of the book itself. *Loyalties* first did this, with Jon Merritt's discussions with the television producer Jock Allicon forming a prelude and afterword to the central tale of Norman Braose, Nesta and Bert Lewis; and its successor, through the narrative of Glyn's search for his grandfather, vastly extends this device. I have written elsewhere of the 'third-generational' structure of feeling that emerges through such frames, the sense in later Williams that cultural and political inheritance takes place from grandparent to grandchild, and that the 'second generation' (Peter Owen's, in effect) is either absent from this process or has actively betrayed it (see *NfN*, 3–11); and this is markedly true of *People of the Black Mountains*. What I want to emphasise here is the 'meta-fictional' function of these narrative frames, the way they raise intriguing formal and ontological questions about the inner stories they cradle. The whole inner narrative of *Loyalties* may after all, in the light of its frame, actually be a television programme or script, that 'utopian' political programme which Jon Merritt knows there is no chance of making under the present social constraints of broadcasting. The more extended framework of Williams's last novel allows such metafictional issues, which centre above all on the nature of history, to be explored in much greater depth — to the point, in fact, where the narrative frame can be the base for a generic hypothesis about the novel.

For in its investigations of history *People of the Black Mountains* seems to me to be most usefully seen as what Linda Hutcheon in her *A Poetics of Postmodernism* calls 'historiographic metafiction', a term which I shall both borrow and reformulate. Linda Hutcheon's book opens with a search for points of fruitful intersection between contemporary theory and artistic practice, on which a 'poetics' might then be constructed, and the most suggestive linkage she finds is the one that preoccupied us in chapter three above.

> The points of overlap that seem most evident to me are those of the paradoxes set up when modernist aesthetic autonomy and self-reflexivity come up against a counterforce in the form of a grounding in the historical, social, and political world. The model I have used is that of postmodern architecture, as theorized by Paolo Portoghesi and Charles Jencks . . . By analogy, what would characterise postmodernism in fiction would be what I here call 'historiographic metafiction', those popular paradoxical works like García Márquez's *One Hundred Years of Solitude*, Grass's *The Tin Drum*, Fowles's *The Maggot (PPM*, ix).

The modernist work, whether it is a building by Le Corbusier or a two-line Imagist poem by Ezra Pound, aspires to 'Make it New' (Pound's slogan). It turns its back on the history of past aesthetic forms and starts all over again from scratch, generating its form from within itself, from the inner logic of its own materials, whether these are steel, glass and reinforced concrete or poetic metaphor. Owing its existence to nothing outside itself, it becomes, in Hutcheon's terms, 'autonomous' and 'self-reflexive', contemplating its own aesthetic navel with an ever more sophisticated self-consciousness. Postmodernism is then, as we have seen, the reassertion of history: the rediscovery of the multiple styles of the past in architecture, or "the 'return' of plot and questions of reference which had been bracketed by late modernist attempts to explode realist conventions" in fiction (*PPM*, xii). But, as I have so often stressed, this is reassertion, and not simple revival or regression, postmodernism rather than anti-modernism. Modernist autonomy and formal self-consciousness are paradoxically preserved even in works which seek determinedly to move beyond them. Postmodern art, Hutcheon maintains, does not choose sides but "lives out the contradiction of giving in to both urges", historiographic *and* metafictional. It is "both intensively self-reflexive and parodic, yet it also attempts to root itself in that which both reflexivity and parody appear to short-circuit: the historical world" (x). Painful though such formal schizophrenia may be, Hutcheon is adamant that there can be no final resolution to it: "there is no dialectic in the postmodern: the self-reflexive remains distinct from its traditionally accepted contrary — the historico-political context in which it is embedded" (x).

Of the metafictional nature of *People of the Black Mountains* there can be no doubt; it first emerges in explicit meditations on history in the narrative frame. A whole series of powerful modernist versions of history are summoned up and trenchantly despatched in the novel's opening pages. The Le Corbusian dream of a *tabula rasa* gets short shrift, as we have seen. But so too does Friedrich Nietzsche's essay on 'The Use and Abuse of History for Life', which is evoked by Glyn: "a long forgetting, it had been argued, was the first condition of history; a discarding of enough for the essentials to be remembered" (I, 10). An encyclopaedic surfeit of history, Nietzsche claimed, was crushing nineteenth-century consciousness; and only a powerful repression of most of it, by the formidable will of an *Übermensch* or superman, would allow us to act vigorously in the present. In the Black Mountains, however, as Williams's novel remarks dryly, "there had indeed been a long forgetting, but of a different kind" (10). Forgetting in this novel, across the long span of its history, is not a conscious act, the assertion of an indomitable Nietzschean will; it is, rather, a matter of having your history stolen from you — your buildings burned, your laws and traditions rewritten, your maps redrawn — by successive waves of invasion and domination. Even the reader is drawn into this process, through the repeated brutal rewriting of place names throughout the text. In theory, perhaps, an ideal reader could juggle in his or her mind the many reinscriptions which any particular spot undergoes in the novel's thirty-seven thousand years: Hawkstone, Menhebog, Glan Bwch, Twmpath. In practice, only a local reader who knows the region as intimately as Elis could possibly do this; and the rest of us, in the inevitable 'forgetting' that is part of reading any long novel, necessarily participate in, not just observe, the repression of the past that characterises any hegemonic social order.

But there are also some versions of modernism which had little truck with the whole notion of 'making it new', themselves harking back to a lost, idealised past in an unsettling 'materialistic' present. The greatest of all such 'historicising' modernisms, Marcel Proust's *A La Recherche du Temps Perdu*, is also alluded to in the opening of *People of the Black Mountains* through reference to the famous madeleine that triggers off the work of memory in its hero: "the mountains were too open, too emphatic, to be reduced to personal recollection: the madeleine, the shout in the street. What moved, if at all, in the moonlit expanse was a common memory, over a common forgetting" (11). That 'common' history might appear to have more relation to the ancient 'organic community' and vegetation myths appealed to in T.S. Eliot's *The Waste Land* than with the poignant but narrowly personal memories of a Virginia Woolf or a Marcel Proust. But whereas Eliot's vision is clearly an idealist construct, using the discoveries of early twentieth-century anthropology to bolster a traditional pastoral Hobbitland of contented peasants, the realist mode of narrative adopted in Williams's forty historical episodes offers to take us 'behind' such constructs, to actual lives and the very feel and texture, moment by moment, of their enduring and enjoying.

The contrast between theoretical construct and 'actual' substance appears on and off throughout Raymond Williams's work, and is yet again reinforced at the start of *People of the Black Mountains*. The cartographic impulse which governs his fiction again comes to the fore, in the two actual maps (past and present) which precede the text of the novel in both volumes, and in the master-map that Glyn contemplates in his grandfather's room, that "large relief model which Elis had built by contours in sliced layers of polystyrene" (I, 7). Yet even this impressive map can be contrasted to its detriment with lived substance: the names and features on the model are accurate enough, but are "very unlike those desolate tops, of heather and sedge and bog cotton and peat pools, of rutted tracks . . . of long featureless ridges and false ridges as you climbed" (7). Here, clearly, is the contrasting of map and "tour", static system and active itinerary, with which we are familiar from *Border Country*; and Glyn's midnight excursus across the mountains is precisely an effort to dissolve the former back into the latter.

If the opposition of map/construct with lived experience were the whole truth of *People of the Black Mountains*, we would indeed have to see it as a realist rather than postmodernist text, as a straightforward historical novel rather than 'historiographical metafiction'. But running alongside the appeal to 'actual substance' in Williams's work is a deep insistence on the role of 'conventions' in our experience; and his most distinctive concept in cultural theory, 'structure of feeling', seeks in its two yoked nouns to hold construct and substance together in a single thought. Even in his spirited defence of realism in *The Long Revolution*, he acknowledges that "the old, naive realism is in any case dead, for it depended on a theory of natural seeing which is now impossible" (*LR*, 315). There is thus no unmediated seeing, no linguistic transparency or 'window on to the world', as George Eliot and Tolstoy tended to assume. Though *People of the Black Mountains* is momentarily tempted by naive realism, it more typically lives on the level of these more sophisticated insights, constantly pondering questions of construct, convention, interpretation of data and linguistic slipperiness even as it vividly gives us its forty historical episodes — many of which, interestingly, foreground the very same hermeneutic issues.

Modernist self-consciousness is thus sustained, as Linda Hutcheon suggested, even in the postmodernist work that seeks to go beyond it. Consider the episode of Karan and the Measurer Dal Mered, which is certainly one of the most deeply felt stories in the first volume. No sooner is this compelling tale told than the novel informs us, in a casual aside that has the full force of Brechtian alienation: "Menvandir. The White Land. The Company of Measurers. It was a possible construction, from the many traces" (I, 237). We must at once, gratingly, switch gears as readers, from realist narration to theoretical self-consciousness and doubt, a shifting of gears which is virtually definitional of 'historiographic metafiction', determined as that is, in Hutcheon's phrase, to live out the contradiction of giving in to both urges. Far from being resolved, the problems of historical representation actually multiply when there are at last written records to be had, rather than the mute archaeological traces of arrow-heads, tools and bones. "After ten thousand generations of conscious life and memory, these written traces, by convention, would be called the beginning of history" (I, 325). It is a memorably angry formulation, rebuking the arrogance of those who deny the dignity of the term 'history' to all that has been lived, suffered and achieved by Marod, Varan, Cara, Incar, Idris, Seril and others across the previous twenty thousand years. And yet, still, it is a condemnation of writing *in* writing, employing the very compromised medium it is aggressively analysing; and the question then arises: can it escape the very processes of domination that it is seeking to define and dislodge?

The answer to this question, for realism, is a resounding: yes. Many kinds of compromised languages circulate in such texts, and their devious rhetorical strategies are often subtly exposed. But there is always one language which escapes the snares of power and rhetoric, and serves as a universal court of appeal at which all lesser languages may be tried and judged: the discourse of omniscient realist narration itself. *People of the Black Mountains*, to its credit, knows that there can be no such disinterestd metalanguage. At certain moments in the novel we enter a Babel of tongues, with Latin, Norman-French, English and Breton all battling for semantic predominance, a Babel enacted by Williams's own text with its liberal usage of local social terms — teyrn, bro, taeog — and its occasional inclusion of entire Norman-French songs. The temptation to appeal against all this to its own lucid, spare prose of realist narration must then be great, but as a work of metafiction rather than fiction, the novel knows that no such option is really open to it. Eager though the book is to challenge the universalising history of the Romans in favour of a place-specific rationality, it also knows that that Roman 'universal account' is "deeply embedded in any language that can be used to define it", including its own (I, 327). You can only challenge a dominant order with the linguistic tools that it has itself provided you with; language is compromised through and through, and yet still the critical challenge to entrenched power must go on being made. At this point, where it is not just particular historical constructions that are being problematised, but the very medium of historical representation, language itself, we sense how closely *People of the Black Mountains* conforms to the genre of historiographical metafiction that Linda Hutcheon has sketched out.

What is history? How can we represent it? Whose history is it? If history is a kind of fiction, are some historical fictions better than others? What does 'better' mean here? Who is competent to decide this? What makes an event 'historical' rather than 'personal' (and vice versa)? Are there laws or regularities in history? If so, how can we discern them? These and other related questions insistently trouble *People of the Black Mountains*, to the point where the initially sharp division between frame and episodes begins to erode, and, in an odd but characteristic metafictional effect, the frame seems to be located within that which it had once bordered, a container now contained by its own contents. One sign of this is the way a 'third-generational' structure of feeling is so often replicated within the historical episodes, Glyn and Elis thus framing a tale that seems composed of Glyns and Elises. The boy Karan and the old Measurer, and the young Christian Nyr and the old Druida Glesni are notable instances, but Iowerth also asserts that "as a son I remember it, but I am prouder to be a grandson" (II, 185), and Conan has married so late in life that he is virtually a grandfather to his own sons. A second sign of this erosion is our sense that certain characters in the narrative coincide with the overall consciousness of the frame itself, becoming Glyns or Elises hundreds or even thousands of years *avant la lettre*: old Karan with his defence of "the sweetness of the place" against Lugon, the ex-monk Conan with his remarkable grasp of historical process, and the brooding figure of the old, blind Tomas, which seems to assert a weight of pain and injustice in history that nothing can subsequently redeem, are all impressive examples of this.

But the third and decisive index of this interbreeding of frame and narrative is the way issues of interpretation, of the very nature and purposes of history, become ever more central to the historical narrative; what this work of historiographical metafiction realistically narrates is, as often as not, metafictional problems in historiography. An early straw in this postmodernist wind is the extended wrangle between Karan and Lugon, where the latter's brisk confidence that "it is a capital offence to threaten a lord" is soon unravelled by Karan's riddling mastery of hermeneutics: "I know also that wisdom must interpret the law" (I, 299). Such metafictional issues are then developed in full in Volume Two, whose very title points us towards them: the Eggs of the Eagle do not just belong to the central spatial fantasy of the nest, but are also opaque signs in the bard Mabon's vision, in need of urgent decoding. A later chapter entitled 'Signs of Vengeance' also highlights semiotic issues. If life and death on a massive scale is at stake in a general Welsh rising against their oppressors, then it is of the utmost urgency to be able to answer such questions as: what is a sign? how do we tell a true sign from a false one? how can we pass from the signifier — a flood, the death of a king — to the signified or meaning? Signs may even signify nothing but the difficulty of their own decipherment, the bafflements that intervene between their material body and any assignable meaning. Lord Glesni interprets the third Egg of the Eagle, with its choking yellow mist, as just such a meta-sign: "it is not an emblem, as the fish is an emblem. It is a vagueness, a shifting, an uncertainty, an obscuring. It is an unseen, unseeable future of our lives" (II, 72). This certainly corresponds to one of the novel's own senses of history when the latter, in its immensity, seems to defeat every effort of human representation: "a history more entangled, more impenetrable than this maze of sheeptracks. Tracks never found, trodden ways not recorded or pursued were necessary to define it" (II, 159).

Yet even within this unmappable process, some historical assertions can be made. Metafiction achieves a negative knowledge, that no representation can ever claim to exhaust the real, and this scepticism may have important social effects. It is a scepticism of which we have good need, since though history may be intensely theoretically problematic, actual histories go on being made and imposed around us all the time. Our rulers are rarely hamstrung by the suspicion of 'grand narratives' that afflicts postmodern intellectuals, but rather energetically cobble together and ruthlessly propound their ideological versions of history and tradition. This process is represented in the novel as the Anglo-Normans concoct their myths of King Arthur to legitimate their own power: "The heathen Saxons broke in to interrupt the true inheritance . . . We resume the legacy of Arthur" (II, 190). "Do you think the Welsh will believe such a story?", inquires Brian Fitzcount, and the answer alas is in general: yes (even if not in the particular instance). For in a powerful passage at the end of Volume One the novel shows how a defeated people that cannot generate its own history may cast even its hope of liberation in the cultural forms of the hegemonic history that oppresses it: "celebrating a resistance . . . in legendary reconstructions, which would give what their rulers now craved — a Roman history, a Roman style of dominant identity which they had never had but could now believe they had lost" (I, 328).

Historiographical metafiction doesn't just bring its corrosive scepticism to bear upon such constructs within the text. As we should expect of a postmodern novel, *People of the Black Mountains* has a rich *inter*textual life, contesting and inverting — even parodying — dominant models of history beyond its frontiers. When King Arthur first appears on the historical scene, Caran remarks dryly, "we shall see if we hear of him again" (II, 82), a poker-faced jest which certainly belongs to the realm of metafiction rather than realism. The Arthur of this novel has precious little in common with the lofty traditional hero, equipped with Round Table and magical sword and sponsored by the Lady of the Lake. 'Artorious', to the shepherds of the Black Mountains, is just another megalomaniac ruler who ruthlessly increases his exactions from ordinary people to finance his grandiose military schemes. The novel ends with another striking intertextual reversal when Sir John Oldcastle, now persecuted by Henry V for his religious convictions, turns up in Olchon and establishes an uneasy alliance with Caradoc — an episode which sombrely 'parodies' or rewrites Shakespeare's account of Henry's banishment of Falstaff (who was based on Oldcastle) in *Henry IV, Part Two*. At the level of the whole novel rather than specific episodes, the "intertext" that *People of the Black Mountains* incessantly invokes, unravels, parodies and refashions is nothing less than the century after century of history-writing which construes the history of the mountains as a conflict of Welsh and English or Viking and Norman; for "one thing this history is not — the resonant clash of unitary peoples" (II, 159). Those old accounts, which we imbibed unthinkingly with our daily milk in junior school, look hopelessly impoverished after the rich deconstruction and reconstruction of histories that this novel carries out.

But if *People of the Black Mountains* is indeed historiographical metafiction, it is, we must admit, an instance of it with a difference — a small difference which, as I have tried to show throughout this volume, makes all the difference. For in accordance with my stress on space, place and geography, on topo-analysis and the socio-spatial dialectic, I'm inclined to reformulate the generic description of Raymond Williams's last novel as 'historico-geographical metafiction'. My analysis of *People of the Black Mountains* began with space, with the womb-nest and its crippling Gothic metamorphoses, and must now end with it. Not, naturally, as a way of denying the issues of history that I have pursued here; as we saw in Chapter Two, the assumption that space and time are

138

rigid opposites is an outmoded 'historicist' one which we should not let ourselves be hampered by. A return to space after the detour of metafictional historiography is, rather, a way of expanding the notion of history, of fully opening it to a socio-spatial dialectic. Williams's last novel is both the most formidably historical and the most overwhelmingly spatial of all his works, a conjunction of interests evident in the actual physical experience of reading the book, which is a highly active, muscular process. For we have not merely to peruse the printed text on the page in front of us but must constantly leap backward to the two maps printed in the front of both volumes, forward to the list of the dates of the stories at the back of the book (in Volume One) and, as the very zone where geography and history most vividly interact, must repeatedly refer across to the list of mutating place names in both volumes. We are compelled to begin a muscular 'itinerary' which mimics Glyn's own; and I cannot imagine a careful reader of these two volumes, even one who has never before ventured to South Wales, not in the end being possessed of a remarkably vivid mental map of the Black Mountains, and a transformed sense of the ways in which, across the millenia, geography and history shape and reshape each other. Glyn's father, we learn, was a historian pure and simple, and this seems related to his 'second-generational' absence from the text. The first and third generations, however, Elis and then Glyn, "had always combined a sustained study of its [the region's] geography and history" (I, 8).

It is tempting, therefore, to apply to both this novel and *Border Country* another generic category that has been thrown up from the world of 'postmodern geographies': *spatial story*. The term is Michel de Certeau's, from his *The Practice of Everyday Life*, where it implies an account of the relations between narrative and space very different from that of Georg Lukács's realism. To lose the ability to narrate, for Lukács, was to plunge into a reified world of sheer space and inert 'description'. For de Certeau, however, the fate of narrative and space is intimately bound together. If one vanishes, so does the other: "where stories are disappearing (or else being reduced to museographical objects), there is a loss of space". For the function of narrative, whether everyday or literary, is in de Certeau's view 'spatial legislation'. The story 'founds spaces'; narrative activity "continues to develop where frontiers and relations with space abroad are concerned'; "like the Roman *fetiales*, stories go in a procession ahead of social practices in order to open a field for them" (*PEL*, 123–5). Only, where narratives normally mark out spaces by establishing frontiers around them, by policing their boundaries, the strange space of Raymond Williams's fiction is not so much a space contained *by* a border as a space *of* the border, that paradoxical 'border country' itself. It is a paradox marked in these 'spatial stories' by their fascination with bridges, where so many of their momentous encounters take place: Peter Owen and Robert Lane on the bridge in Port Meadow in *Second Generation*, Peter and Matthew Price on the bridge at Pontafren in *Manod* ("You feel it here, do you? . . . Something different", *M*, 97), Norman and Emma Braose at a crucial turning point in the former's political career in *Loyalties* ("it came at last, on the little bridge over the river", *L*, 106), or Tami squatting on a bridge in *People of the Black Mountains* and watching the first savage raiders, the 'Devils', enter his homeland in 1050 B.C. For which space does a bridge belong to? This bank? That bank? Both? Neither?

In 1984 Raymond Williams argued that "a new theory of socialism must now centrally involve *place*" (*RH*, 242), thereby lending his authority to those calls for a 'postmodern geography' which we examined in Chapter Two. There are many pointers as to what this 'socialism of place' would look like in his later social writings, and some oblique anticipations of this 'spatial turn' in his earlier ones. But our major resource for eliciting a fullscale postmodern socialist geography from Williams's work is without doubt that impressive series of 'spatial stories' from *Border Country* to *People of the Black Mountains*. For in these novels socio-spatial issues are explored with an immediacy and thoroughness that doesn't begin to surface in the theoretical writings until years later. We must, then, take very seriously the author's claim that it was in writing his fiction that he learnt how to become the cultural theorist he so eminently was. But if we do take this claim on board, we shall be required, in reading and re-reading these novels, to reformulate our sense of what cultural theory in Williams actually meant. The intricate, often disturbing textuality of his novels is still neglected in nearly all accounts of Raymond Williams — as, necessarily, are the new theoretical insights to which that textuality ultimately points us. Yet it is only a reading of that fiction or, better, a reading of it in the contexts of postmodernism which can explain why Williams is both so local and so international a writer, rooted in his native landscape like few other intellectuals this century and yet intervening, with full authority, in all the great cultural and political debates of our epoch. For the last spatial paradox in Raymond Williams is also the one I opened this book with: the paradox that the most minute and most overarching of spaces, the region and the global system, pass strangely into and out of each other, bypassing the territory of the old nation-state, the 'Yookay' as *Towards 2000* derisively terms it. But that a few square miles of actual Welsh border country now constitute a spatial vortex through which our entire contemporary world in one way or another must pass, so that the multinational postmodernist city 'Manod' and the moribund actual village Manod bafflingly inhabit the same space — this is a paradox that only a 'postmodern novelist' who was simultaneously a 'postmodern geographer' could know and communicate.

Bibliography

1. Raymond Williams's Novels

Border Country (London: Hogarth Press, 1988). First published 1960.
Second Generation (London: Hogarth Press, 1988). First published 1964.
The Volunteers (London: Hogarth Press, 1985). First published 1978.
The Fight for Manod (London: Hogarth Press, 1988). First published 1979.
Loyalties (London: Hogarth Press, 1989). First published 1985.
People of the Black Mountains.
   1. *The Beginning* (London: Chatto and Windus, 1989).
   2. *The Eggs of the Eagle* (London: Chatto and Windus, 1990).

2. Raymond Williams's Non-Fiction

Drama from Ibsen to Eliot (London: Chatto and Windus, 1952) = *DIE*.
Culture and Society: 1780–1950 (London: Chatto and Windus, 1958) = *CS*.
The Long Revolution (Harmondsworth: Pelican Books, 1965) = *LR*. First published 1961.
The English Novel from Dickens to Lawrence (London: Chatto and Windus, 1970) = *EN*.
The Country and the City (St Albans, Herts: Paladin, 1975) = *CC*. First published 1973.
Television: Technology and Cultural Form (London: Fontana/Collins, 1974) = *TTCF*.
Politics and Letters: Interviews u:.1 New Left Review (London: New Left Books, 1979) = *PL*.
Towards 2000 (London: Chatto and Windus, 1983).
Writing in Society (London: Verso, 1984) = *WS*.
Raymond Williams on Television: Selected Writings, edited by Alan O'Connor (London: Routledge, 1989) = *RWT*.
Resources of Hope: Culture, Democracy, Socialism, edited by Robin Gable (London: Verso, 1989) = *RH*.
What I Came To Say, edited by Francis Mulhern (London: Hutchinson, 1989) = *WICS*.

Writers in Conversation: Raymond Williams with Michael Ignatieff (ICA Video).

III. Other Works Used

Bachelard, Gaston, *The Poetics of Space*, translated by M. Jolas (Beacon Paperback, 1969) = *PS*.

Baudrillard, Jean, *Selected Writings*, edited by Mark Poster (Oxford: Polity Press, 1988) = *SW*.

de Certeau, Michel, *The Practice of Everyday Life*, translated by Steven Rendall (Berkeley: University of California Press, 1984) = *PEL*.

Foucault, Michel, 'Of Other Spaces', *Diacritics* no. 16 (1987), pp. 22–27 = 'OOS'.

Eagleton, Terry, ed., *Raymond Williams: Critical Perspectives* (Oxford: Polity Press, 1989) = *RWCP*.

Harvey, David, *The Condition of Postmodernity* (Oxford: Basil Blackwell, 1989) = *CPM*.

Hutcheon, Linda, *A Poetics of Postmodernism: History, Theory, Fiction* (London: Routledge, 1988) = *PPM*.

Ibsen, Henrik, *Plays: Four*, translated by Michael Meyer (London: Eyre Methuen, 1980) = *P*.

Jameson, Fredric, 'Cognitive Mapping', in *Marxism and the Interpretation of Culture*, edited by Cary Nelson and Lawrence Grossberg (London: Macmillan, 1988) = 'CM'.

—— 'Postmodernism, or the Cultural Logic of Late Capitalism', *New Left Review* no. 146 (July/August 1984), pp. 53–92 = 'PCL'.

—— 'Postmodernism and Utopia", in *Utopia Post Utopia* (Cambridge, Massachusetts: MIT Press, 1988) = "PU".

—— 'Rimbaud and the Spatial Text', in *Rewriting Literary History*, edited by Tak-Wai Wong and M.A. Abbas (Hong Kong University Press, 1984) = 'RST'.

Jencks, Charles, *The Language of Post-Modern Architecture*, revised edition (London, 1978) = *LPA*.

Lévi-Strauss, Claude, *Structural Anthropology*, translated by Claire Jacobson and Brooke Grundfest Schoepf (London, 1969) = *SA*.

Lukács, Georg, *Writer and Critic*, translated by Arthur Kahn (London: Merlin Press, 1978) = *WC*.

Lyotard, Jean-François, *The Postmodern Condition: A Report on Knowledge*, translated by Geoff Bennington and Brian Massumi (Manchester: Manchester University Press, 1984) = *PC*.

McHale, Brian, *Postmodernist fiction*, (London: Methuen, 1987) = *PF*.

O'Connor, Alan, *Raymond Williams: Writing, Culture, Politics* (Oxford: Blackwells, 1989) = *RW:WCP*.

Pinkney, Tony, ed., *News from Nowhere* no.6, special issue on 'Raymond Williams: Third Generation', February 1989 = *NFN*.

Ross, Kristin, *The Emergence of Social Space: Rimbaud and the Paris Commune* (London: Macmillan, 1988).

143

Soja, Edward, *Postmodern Geographies: The Reassertion of Space in Critical Social Theory* (London: Verso, 1989) = *PG*.

Ward, J.P., *Raymond Williams*, 'Writers of Wales' (University of Wales Press, 1981).

—— 'Raymond Williams as Inhabitant: The Border Trilogy', *New Welsh Review* vol. 1, no. 2 (Autumn 1988), pp. 23–27 = 'RWI'.